RUGBY
Anecdotes, records and polemics

GRAHAM ADIN

Foreword

In rugby, as in other domains, the great and the small of history often merged to create moments that left their mark on people's minds.

During discussions between Rugger enthusiasts, I've noticed that many don't know, or have forgotten, the ins and outs of certain famous episodes. As the years go by, images become foggy, souvenirs become muddled and memories fade.

What's more, certain players, facts and anecdotes have mysteriously, and unjustly, fallen into oblivion.

Without claiming to be exhaustive, but providing as much detail as possible, the stories that follow attempt to remedy this. These 32 articles are independent of each other and can be read in any order.

For younger readers who have not lived through these periods, I have taken great pleasure in describing the context in which each situation took place. It's important to bring these moments, these records, these scandals and these people with exceptional careers to the attention of as many enthusiasts as possible. Not to hammer home the point that 'it was better before', but so that we don't forget that rugby was before being.

This publication is the fruit of extensive documentation and cross-referencing of information from a variety of sources. And because we have to give credit where credit is due, I would like to thank them by quoting them below:

20minutes.fr (website)
Actu.fr (website)
BBC (website)
BFM (website)
Benchmark: Life, laughter and the law (book) O. Popplewell
Boudulemag.com (website)
Branchezrugby.fr (website)
Businesslive.co.za (website)
Classic-Wallabies (website)
Courrier International (website)
Eden Park
Enquête Faits Divers (Youtube channel)
ESPN.co.uk (website)
FFR.fr (website)
France24.com (website)
France 3 Occitanie (website)
Huffingtonpost (website and newspaper)
Inews.com (website)
IOL (website)
La Depêche (website and newspaper)
Le Figaro (website and newspaper)
La Montagne (website and newspaper)
Le journal de Saône et Loire (website)
Le Monde (website and newspaper)
Le Parisien (website and newspaper)

L'Equipe (website and newspaper)
Libération (website and newspaper)
Midi Olympique (website and newspaper)
Nzherald.co.nz (website and newspaper)
OpenEdition Books (website)
RMC (website)
Ruck n'maul (blog)
RugbyBack (Youtube channel)
Rugbyrama (website)
Rugbyrocks (website)
Rugby365 (website)
South China Morning Post (website and newspaper)
Sport24.co.za (website)
Sporting-heroes.net (website)
Sport 24 Le Figaro (website)
Stuff.co.nz (website)
Sud Ouest (website)
Surlatouche.fr (website)
The Daily Telegraph (website and newspaper)
The Guardian (website and newspaper)
The Independent (website and newspaper)
Thesouthafrican (website)
The Irish Time (website and newspaper)
The Sidney Morning Herald (website and newspaper)
The Times (website and newspaper)
The42.ie (website)
Wales Online (website)
Wikipedia (website)
Worldrugbycup.com (website)

Contents

Foreword III

1 – Rugby and Revolution 1

2 – 11 February 2007: Rugby at Croke Park! 7

3 – Samoa: Additional time for stoppages! 9

4 – 1962: Béziers first European champion 17

5 – Nobody is perfect 21

6 – 2009: The Bastareaud case 33

7 – 1997: Welcome to the Wild South 41

8 – Nightmare at Kamp Staaldraad 49

9 – 2009: A bloody wink 57

10.1 – Marc Cécillon: The stainless band leader 67

10.2 – Marc Cécillon: How anonymity can be a road to hell 85

11 – 1995: The All Blacks go pale 107

12 – Expreso de medianoche: Willie Anderson 111

13 – Are the French frightening? 119

14 – Naas Botha, a 1000-faceted diamond 127

15 – Broken destinies 131

16 – Ireland's two national anthems 141

17 – Inevitable Professionalisation 145

17.1 – Birth of the parent institution: IRFB 147

17.2 – The XIII as a counterweight to the XV: in the northern hemisphere. 153

17.3 – The XIII as a counterweight to the XV: in the southern hemisphere. 169

17.4 – Hypocrisy and sanctions 181

17.5 – 1995: The change, please! 191

18 – The Argentinian Bajadita 203

19 – The extraordinary life of Mr Mayor 207

20 – 1974: The first official streaker 213

21 – 1991: When the French national team almost went on strike! 221

22 – Lawrence Dallaglio: The weaknesses of a champion 225

23 – 1986: The battle of Nantes 237

24 – 1973: A 5 Nations Championship with no losers... and no winners 259

25 – Record in the land of the rising sun 263

26 – 24 February 2007: The English "back" at Croke Park 269

27 – 1990: The world's most beautiful anthem is born 273

1

Rugby and Revolution

The qualities of team spirit, tenacity and commitment are as common to rugby players as they are to warriors who win major battles. So it's not surprising to learn that Ernesto Che Guevara, the man who carried off several popular revolutions in South America, was also an outstanding wing three-quarter. Was he a revolutionary who played rugby or a rugbyman who led the revolt?

Ernesto Guevara de la Serna was born in 1928 in Rosario, Argentina, into a fairly well-to-do family. When he was just two years old, doctors diagnosed Ernesto with severe asthma. Over the next two years, they administered a number of treatments to cure his chronic ailment, but to no avail. The Guevara family was then advised to move to a region with a less polluted atmosphere. The family settled temporarily in Cordoba, in the centre-north of the country.

According to the principles of the Argentinian upper class, a healthy mind can only develop in a healthy body.

Growing up, Ernesto tried his hand at many sporting activities, such as hiking, football (as a goalkeeper), swimming and golf. But it was his lifelong friend Alberto Granado, who would accompany him on his future tribulations, who introduced him to rugby.

At the age of 14, Guevara showed an interest in the oval ball. Stunted in appearance, and more than ever plagued by violent asthma attacks, the local teams refused to play him. Determined, Ernesto asked his friend Tomas Granado to put him in touch with his brother Alberto, who played for and coached Estudiantes de Cordoba.

'I want to play rugby', exclaimed Guevara to Alberto Granado, 6 years his senior, during their conversation. At first hesitant, then caught up by his personal story, the man who played number 9 in the Estudiantes de Cordoba's first team finally agreed to take the future Che under his wing. 'As I, too, had suffered discrimination because I was skinny and short-legged, I said to him: 'I'm going to teach you'. And he learned.'

Introduced to the oval ball, Ernesto quickly earned his place in the Estudiante's first team on the left wing. He first attracted attention for his habit of taking a dose of Ventolin every 15 minutes, then returning to his position as if nothing had happened. But it is really his rugby skills that most impressed his team-mates. 'He was a talented, extremely intelligent lad,' said Francisco Ventura, one of his playing partners.

Granado was equally effusive in his praise of his winger's strengths: 'He had an excellent tackle, at elbow height. Fuser's will to defend was terrible.' The nickname 'Fuser' was quickly given to Ernesto. It's a contraction of *Furibundo de la Serna* (*Furious Serna*). Anecdotally, Fuser is also the name of a set play developed by the two partners in crime, Guevara and Granado: 'When I called out "Fuser" at the scrum exit, close to the opposition goal line, it meant that I was going to fake the pass on the open side, but in fact pass the ball between my legs to Ernesto, who had come to the axis of the scrum. He scored a lot of tries that way,' recalled the former No 9. And he added: 'He would try crazy things, always knowing what he was doing and where he was going. He never lost a ball, so to speak.'

In 1947, the Guevara family moved to Buenos Aires, the Argentinian capital. Ernesto started studying medicine there. While he flourished in various fields, such as photography, reading and writing, his heart remained devoted to rugby. So it was only natural that he joined the San Isidro Club, presided over by his uncle, Martinez Castro.

His father's reluctance to take up the sport, backed up by the doctors, was a thorn in his side. Although admiring, the Guevara patriarch, concerned to see his son organized such a 'violent and exhausting' sport, tried to make him see reason. 'The doctors told me that this sport was almost suicidal for my son, that his heart couldn't take it. One day, I told him so, and he replied: 'Dad, I love rugby, and even if I have to die playing it, I'm going to keep on doing it.' Faced with such stubbornness, I decided to use other methods.'

Guevara's father then went to his brother-in-law, the president of the San Isidro Club, and managed to get his son excluded from the team. Disgusted and furious, Ernesto defied the patriarchal interdict and joined a neighbouring club, Ypora Rugby Club. He briefly played there before joining the Atalaya Polo Club.

Legend has it that Che, the leader of revolutions, played scrum-half, the ideal position for leading men. In reality, 'he was more of a centre three-quarter', recalled a former team-mate, Diégo Bonadeo. Because of his snub nose, his fierce fighting spirit and his deliberately unkempt style, Ernesto Guevara found himself saddled with a new nickname in those years: El Chancho (The Pig).

On 28 August and 4 September 1949, Guevara, father and son, accompanied by Alberto Granado, attended the matches between the Argentine national team and the French XV. Led by René Crabos, the latter crossed the equator for the first time. Les Bleus was caught by surprise by a resilient and combative local team, who only lost 5-0, then 12-3. Ernesto Guevara was also pleasantly surprised. More than that, he was thrilled. He loved the clash of styles between the Argentinian forward's play and the spread game played by the French.

Described as a 'beautiful game', the French style was highlighted in articles published in 1951 in the weekly magazine Tackle, Argentina's first rugby magazine. The articles were written by a certain Chancho, who shortly afterwards changed his author's name to Chang-Cho.

It turns out that Chang-Cho was none other than Guevara himself, who co-founded Tackle. The magazine, whose original copies are now worth a fortune, published just 11 issues between 5 May and 28 July 1951.

In the months that followed, Ernesto's destiny would take a historic turn, this time earning him the undying nickname of Che. Diego Bonadeo recalled an anecdote that took place during the inter-university games, in which Guevara's team was taking part: 'One guy asked why Guevara wasn't playing, and another replied: "He's fighting a revolution in Panama"'.

Che and his friend Granado were not in the field. They decided to get on a motorbike (a Norton 500), nicknamed Poderosa, and travel around

South America. 'It was because of our rugby friendship, this brotherhood of arms, that Ernesto and I set off together on an expedition to Venezuela', recalled Alberto thirty years later. During this first trip, where they came into close contact with poverty, the first revolutionary ideas germinated in their minds.

The rest is part of the great history of the two men, recounted in the notebook 'Notas de viaje', which has served as the basis for many films on the legend of Che.

Ernesto Guevara's destiny and ideological adventure then took him to Cuba, where he took part in Fidel Castro's rise to power. During these years, he was forced to quench his thirst for sport by playing baseball, as rugby culture was non-existent on the island. However, he still had vivid memories of playing rugby. 'When I saw him in Cuba before he left for his destiny in Bolivia, we used to talk about our youth. Above all, it had a name: rugby', declared Alberto Granado in 1987. The latter settled in Cuba following the revolution. He would become a biochemist and would found the medical school of Santiago de Cuba.

Granado himself remained convinced that rugby played a major role in the fate of the man he knew as a frail pre-adolescent and who went on to become the famous Che: 'He had courage, pugnacity, tenacity, willpower, all the qualities that real men possess. Rugby enabled him to develop them and make him more self-confident.'

2

11 February 2007: Rugby at Croke Park!

On 11th February 2007, Ireland hosted France on day 2 of the 6 Nations Championship (France won 17-20). With Dublin's legendary Lansdowne Road stadium under renovation, the match was being played at Croke Park. It was a historic day, as the stadium had not seen a rugby match for almost a hundred years. This was not a question of capacity or any other standard but rather of a wound that the Irish were carrying with them for almost a century.

21st November 1920. At the height of the Irish War of Independence, the IRA (Irish Republican Army), under the command of Michael Collins, simultaneously assassinated 14 British agents or informers and wounded 6 others.

On the same day, a Gaelic football match between Dublin and Tipperary was held at Croke Park. 15,000 people were packed into the stadium, delighted to see the spectacle that was about to take place. But just as the teams were taking to the field, British auxiliary troops entered the arena, claiming to have located some of the perpetrators of the killings that had taken place that morning.

According to initial reports at the time, the British then came under fire. They spotted their assailants, allegedly armed with revolvers, scattered around the stands. Their response was immediate: they fired into the crowd. The result: 14 people were killed and nearly 65 injured. The victims included 2 children aged 10 and 11, as well as a player present on the pitch, Michael Hogan.

An enquiry was opened. No revolver was found at the scene. Then, after some thought, the British soldiers doubted whether they had been attacked with firearms. It soon transpired that the massacre was nothing more than a reprisal against the local population. Nothing more than blind revenge in response to the murders of the British agents.

This day has since been given the evocative name of Bloody Sunday, not to be confused with another fateful day of the same name (on 30th January 1972, the British army also opened fire on the population of Derry in Northern Ireland).

By 1920, Croke Park had already not hosted a rugby match for almost fifteen years. After the events of 21st November, the GAA, the Irish Gaelic Football Association, which owns the arena, decided that the grass would only be used for Gaelic football matches. This means that no British sports such as rugby or football could be played there.

It was not until over 100 years later, and almost 87 years after Bloody Sunday, that rugby made its return to Croke Park. French hooker Raphaël Ibanez scored the first try of the match. After the match, he declared with great distinction: 'Am I the first to score at Croke Park? I would have preferred it to be an Irishman who did it.'

3

Samoa: Additional time for stoppages!

Famous for his devastating tackles, which earned him the nickname of 'The Chiropractor', Samoan winger or centre Brian Lima had a rich rugby journey. His nickname came from Gordon Hunter, his coach when he played for Otago: 'Every time he (Brian) tackled someone, you could hear the crack of a bone being put back into place by his opponent!' He took advantage of the turnaround brought about by the professionalisation of Rugger to fill his trophy cabinet and was a records holder for many years.

Born on 25th January 1972 in Apia, the capital of Samoa, Brian Pala Lima made his debut in top-level rugby in 1990, in his homeland, with the Marist Saint Joseph club. Powerful and uncompromising in defence, he foreshadowed the future development of the winger and centre three-quarter positions. In the years that followed, physical players would gradually overtake more modest stature. Immediately spotted by Su'a Peter Schuster, the executive director of the Samoan federation, he integrated the Manu Samoa squad, which was preparing for its first participation in a World Cup.

On 6th October 1991, the Samoan archipelago entered the first world competition in its history. At the age of 19 years and 255 days, winger Brian Lima became the youngest player ever to play in a World Cup. This record would not be beaten until 2007 by American Thretton Palamo. The Samoans, reputed to be difficult to play against, revealed themselves to the world of rugby. They brought with them their speciality: destructive chest tackles that bring their opponents to a screeching halt. Lima already excelled in this exercise, which would remain his trademark throughout his years at the highest level.

Led by their fiery spirit, the islanders first beat a Welsh team in a massive period of doubt. They then narrowly lost out to the Australians but went on to defeat the Argentinians. Their superb run came to an end in the quarter-final when they were beaten 28-6 by Scotland. During the tournament, the youngest winger ever to play in a World Cup scored twice.

Noticed by scouts, he joined Auckland in 1992 to play in the New Zealand Domestic Championship. Between 1992 and 1996, however, he kept his licence with his formative club, Marist Saint Joseph's, which he rejoined when he was not playing in New Zealand.

In 1995, during the World Cup in South Africa, the specialists were eagerly awaiting the Polynesian archipelago's players. They did not disappoint and, as expected, put on a great show. They lost in the quarter-final to eventual champions South Africa. Brian Lima, under close scrutiny, delivered a performance to match the occasion, with increasingly frenetic tackles and 2 tries scored.

In 1996, with the creation of the Super 12, history accelerated for the truculent Polynesian winger. He was selected to play for the Otago Highlanders, then for the Auckland Blues franchise in 1997 and 1998, with whom he won the Super 12 in 1997. In 1999, he was back with the Otago Highlanders, who reached the final of the flagship competition.

1999 was also the year of an important milestone for rugby: the fourth World Cup, which was played in France and the British Isles. At just 27, Lima was already contesting his third-world tournament! He ran 3 tries and helped Samoa beat Wales again in the group stage. Then the adventure stopped in the play-off against Scotland, once again.

After the world championships, The Chiropractor seized the opportunity to officiate in the northern hemisphere, accepting an offer from Stade Français. He would be part of the extended squad that won the Brennus Shield in 2000. However, failing to impose himself in the face of fierce competition, the Parisian club released him in 2001.

His European adventure continued in Wales with the Black and Whites of Swansea RFC. This was his chance to add a Welsh championship title to his list of honours.

As one season followed another, the 2003 World Cup loomed on the horizon. Having become a leader and symbol of the Samoan national team, Lima was naturally chosen to take part. Along with England's Jason Leonard and Canada's Al Charron, the Samoan equalled the record previously held by another Canadian, Gareth Rees; together, they formed the very select circle of players to have played in four World Cups. In top form against South Africa, he administered a huge tumbled tackle to fly-half Derick Hougaard, which remains etched in the memory and is still one of the most viewed tackle videos on the Net!

Manu Samoa struggled to get out of the group stage that year. Brian, on the other hand, returned to a Pacific island – Japan – by signing up with the Secom club. Observers assumed that he was quietly preparing for the end of his career. Not so!

After two high-profile appearances for the Pacific Islanders (a selection of the best Polynesian players), The Chiropractor was invited to join the southern hemisphere team in 2005. The team was formed for a charity match against a selection of northerners in aid of the victims of the 2004 tsunami. His remarkable performance attracted the attention of the province of Munster. With a shortage of three-quarters, the Irish offered him a 3-month trial. The Pacific deboner was back in the saddle for a major new challenge!

Unfortunately, fate dealt him a bad hand. He got injured as soon as he arrived in Ireland and would never play for Munster. Lima was certainly disappointed but in no way despondent, as his name found its way onto the shortlist of a number of other European clubs.

Bristol Bears won the negotiations and incorporated the bloodthirsty tackler into their ranks in 2005 for two seasons. Building on their excellent momentum, the English club disputed a Premiership semi-final in 2007, losing to Leicester.

Although he turned 35 in 2007, the versatile Samoan backward was still a key member of his national team. So it's only natural that he should make history for a second time, becoming the first player to play in five World Cups. This time, he assured us, it would be the last! As the icing on the record cake, Brian Lima can also boast of having scored tries in four editions of the competition!

Unfortunately, just like a gangster's last missed trick before going to retirement, things didn't work out for the best. First of all, Samoa lost 59-7 to the Springboks. The second game against neighbours Tonga, whom they had crushed 50-3 in their warm-up match, ended in a 15-19 defeat. As a result, they would have to overturn England to have any hope of qualifying.

It was during this match against the Red Roses (lost 44-22) that Brian Lima's international career would come to an unfortunate end. In the 42nd minute, England fly-half Wilkinson launched an attack inside Samoa's 30 metres. He found himself up against The Chiropractor, who, as usual, aimed at his opponent's plexus. But the target proved to be off, and Wilko was mowed down by a terrible tumbling stiff-arm tackle. Referee Alan Lewis awarded a penalty to the English side and gave a stern reprimand to the Samoan.

But the matter did not end there, and following the match, the Disciplinary Committee called Lima in for the dangerous tackle. For the player, who was very aggressive in defence but who had never shown any violent behaviour and who had never even been cited, the penalty fell like a knife: a 3-week suspension.

The final group match against the United States (won 25-21) was played without the emblematic Lima, depriving him of a fond farewell to the grass, a last hurrah in his beloved colours, and an exit worthy of a player of his standing. At the end of the World Cup, he withdrew from the game, as announced, simply because, as he puts it, 'his body was showing him it was time to stop'.

After wearing the jersey of his national team for more than 17 years, Brian Lima's record is unequivocal: 64 international caps – a national record – (remember that Samoa does not play major competitions every year), 29 tries scored, 5 World Cups contested and tries scored in 4 of these competitions. As for what can't be quantified, he had an incalculable number of crash tackles distributed to his opponents all over the globe, as well as an almost divine aura within his national team.

What are the secrets of such longevity? The player himself humbly answered this question shortly after his retirement: 'I was lucky to start young and to have been spared major injuries'.

Su'a Peter Schuster, the person who discovered 'the man who made the Samoans so proud', puts it another way: 'His humility in the face of his success impressed me, and his commitment to his country can never be called into question. In the morning, while the other players are asleep, Brian goes for a run. And at the end of training, when the others return to the changing room, he sets himself some sprinting sessions.' And Lilomaiava Taufusi Salesa, the great Samoan coach, adds: 'There were a lot of good players, certainly better than Brian, but his commitment and desire to improve made him an extraordinary player.'

As a crowning point, Brian Lima was inducted into the IRB Hall of Fame in 2011. He is still one of the few members not from a major rugby nation.

There is just one cloud in the star-studded sky of Samoa's most capped player. In 2014, he appeared in court for beating up his ex-wife, Sina, and threatening to kill people who tried to intervene. Although he faced up to seven years in prison, he was only sentenced to two years probation, with an obligation to undergo psychiatric treatment. And then nothing more. Back to near anonymity for The Chiropractor.

In 2015, his record of appearances at five World Cups was equalled by Italy's Mauro Bergamasco and Romania's Ovidiu Tonita (although Tonita did not play a single match in 1999).

In August 2020, Brian Lima returned to the limelight. He was appointed coach of his country's 7-a-side rugby team, with the task of restoring a team in decline to its former glory. We can only hope that this undertaking will be crowned with success and that Dr Lima will be able to pass on his secrets of longevity and his gift for chiropractic to the young Samoan rugby team.

4

1962: Béziers first European champion

When one thinks of the first European Club Cup, the 1995/96 edition of the Heineken Cup, won by Stade Toulousain, immediately springs to mind. However, long before that, in the 1960s, a European competition had been tried out under the aegis of FIRA. 4 FIRA European Champion Clubs' Cups were held, and each of them saw a French club reach the final. However, only one of them brought home the trophy: AS Béziers.

In 1931, the French Rugby Federation was excluded from the 5 Nations Championship. The cause of the ban was violence during matches involving the French national team, as well as suspicions that amateurism, the golden rule of rugby at the time, was not being respected. As a result, all French teams were banned from playing against a nation belonging to the IRFB. The IRFB is an organisation created at the end of the 19th century that federates most of the major nations.

Under the impetus of France, FIRA (Fédération Internationale de Rugby Amateur) was formed in 1934. Its main mission was to promote and develop rugby in nations not affiliated with the IRFB. Initially made up of federations from European countries, including Germany, Italy, Belgium, Portugal, Romania and Holland, FIRA rapidly extended its influence. First in Europe, then around the world.

In 1961, the FIRA board decided that, as was the case in football for some years, a European competition should be held. In theory, it would bring together the European champion clubs of their respective countries. The idea has been rightly seen as a significant step forward in the promotion of rugby.

No sooner said than done. The first European Champion Clubs' Cup was organised in 1962. The competition would be played entirely in Romania in the format of a tournament.

6 teams, some of which would make you smile at the moment, had accepted the invitation: the Belgians from SCA Bruxelles, the Germans from SV 08 Ricklingen, the Dutch from RC Hilversum, the Romanians from Grivita Bucarest and the Moroccans from ASPTT Rabat. France was represented by AS Béziers, led by Dedieu and Danos, winners of the Brennus Shield last season. The organisers were not averse to holding grudges, and some British clubs were also invited to take part. They all declined to take part in the competition on the grounds that such participation would breach the principle of non-professionalism. It's clear that amateurism was no laughing matter in the British Isles!

On 24th June 1962, in a Dinamo stadium in Bucharest with a spectator turnout of some 20,000, AS Béziers beat local side Grivita 11-3 in the final. The Hérault rugby club thus became the first to win a European crown!

SU Agen, French champions in 1961/62, declined the invitation for the next edition for some unknown reason. Instead, FC Grenoble would represent France at the tournament. However, after losing the final, Grenoble was unable to join the Béziers team at the European champions' table.

The following season would certainly be the most successful for the competition, which was expanding. Among others, it welcomed Italian club Rovigo and Czech side Spartak Prague. Grivita Bucharest, playing at home, shone by beating RUC Casablanca 27-0 in the quarter-finals, then TSV Victoria Linden (Hanover) 18-3 in the semi-finals. The Romanians were crowned champions against Mont-de-Marsan, the reigning French champions (winning the final 10-0). The match would not go the distance, as the referee decided to stop the game at the start of the second half. André Boniface, who was sent off and refused to leave the pitch, disqualified his team.

Despite some promising first editions, the future of the European Champion Clubs' Cup looked bleak. Due to a lack of funds, it could not be held during the 1964/65 season. It did, however, return the following season, in a scaled-down version, for a last-ditch effort.

In what would be the last tournament, only 4 teams were competing, including SU Agen. A new feature was that the final, which pits Dinamo Bucharest against Agen, was being played over two legs (first and return matches).

SUA hosted the first leg at the Stade Armandie on 25 December 1966 on a pitch that turned into a real quagmire. With Michel Sitjar on fire and scoring 3 tries, the Frenches won 12-0 and began dreaming of becoming European champions.

The return match was to be played in Romania, and the stakes go far beyond sport. The current political regime had hijacked the event and was using it as a propaganda tool. Dinamo literally had no right to lose and would use any means necessary to achieve their goal.

In the week leading up to the final, Romanian coach Dumitru Ionescu was sent to France incognito to analyse in depth Agen's game. Also, as fate would have it, the referee appointed to blow the whistle was Romanian.

The second part of this final took place on 9th June 1967 in Bucharest. The Agen team was caught in an ambush. The game was marred by violence and low blows. Lock Jacques Fort recalled: "During the first half, we stuck together, but after that, it became dangerous."

Dinamo won 18-0 and remained the last reigning European champions until 1995. The European Champion Clubs' Cup was never played again.

However, FIRA continued to expand its membership over the following decades before gradually coming under the authority of the International Rugby Board in the 1990s. Today, it continues to promote rugby by organising more modest competitions.

Admittedly, this first version of the European Cup did not last long and did not bring together all the top clubs (some of whom did not even play in Europe!). But, given the financial and material resources available at the time, holding it for 4 seasons was an exceptional achievement. It was the work of passionate, visionary people who wanted to promote and develop rugby across borders at a time when this was rarely done.

5

Nobody is perfect

What do Irishmen Murphy O'Connor, Keith Wood, and Australian John Eales have in common?

All three played in the forward's pack. Yes, but it doesn't stop there. They also showed a liking for kicking game, an unusual skill for forwards. While Keith Wood excelled at probing kicks, O'Connor and Eales were real scorers, turning games on their feet. To this day, the Australian is the forward with the most points scored at both the national and international level.

Beyond that, John Eales literally sublimated the lock position. Exemplary as Captain Courage of the Wallabies, he won every title an Australian player could win. The Queensland giant had a perfect career in every aspect.

Born on 27th June 1970 in Brisbane, Australia, John Eales attended Marist College Ashgrove. Nature offered him a physique that predisposed him to sporting activities. In his youth, he played cricket at an excellent level. He also enjoyed playing rugby as a side sport.

His art studies, with a specialisation in psychology, led him to Queensland University. Initially, he still played cricket, but later gave up the sport to devote himself entirely to rugby.

In 1989, he signed for Brothers Old Boys, a club competing in the Queensland Championship. His height (2m – 6'7 inches) logically led him to play as a forward. He decides to settle into the second row.

His first season was brilliant and put the Eales star into orbit. In 1990, less than a year after joining the Brothers Old Boys, he was called up by the Queensland Reds, the selection of the province's best players.

The recent retirement of Bill Campbell has left a vacancy in the Reds' second row.

Fast, skilful, solid on impact and, above all, an outstanding jumper, Eales didn't have to force his talent to make it his own. At just 20 years of age, observers were already predicting a glittering career for him. The sharp eye of England's Paul Ackford immediately spotted the young Australian's huge potential. Highlighting his athletic qualities, he declared that he had the ability to make space for himself in claustrophobic places.

The promising second-rower soon demonstrates that those who praised him were right. In July 1991, a month after his 21st birthday, coach Bob Dwyer threw him into the deep end. Australia thrashed a drifting Welsh side 63-6. Apart from a few shortcomings in the scrum and in his movement, John Eales produced a perfect copy. Muscular and skilful, he confirmed his excellent abilities as a jumper, catching 13 of the 20 balls won by his lineout.

The following week, the Wallabies, already in the running for the Bledisloe Cup, made short work of the English, who had won the Grand Slam a few months earlier. John outrageously dominated his opposite number, Martin Bayfield. Colin Meads, the legendary All Black, was blown away by the performance. He believed that Eales 'could play anywhere and would be very good at it for the next ten years'. With this, the Australian had just earned his place at the 1991 World Cup.

The Wallabies were experiencing difficulties in finding the right fuel at the start of the World Cup. Bob Dwyer attempted to reshuffle his pack and decided to use Eales in number 8. After being stunned by Argentina and then struggling to overcome Samoa, the Australians hit the ground running against Wales in their final group match. John Eales returned to the second row, and with his mate Rod McCall, they won 28 of the 30 throws played! The rest was taken care of by two other living legends. Lynagh was precise in his goal attempts, while Campese set the game alight.

A thrilling quarter-final won over Ireland at Lansdowne Road, thanks to a last-minute try from Lynagh (again), finally cemented the Wallaby squad. A week later, against the All Blacks, it was Campese who sped up the match. England was the last team to face Australia in their quest for the Webb Ellis Cup. And Eales would be back in the news.

As usual, he was imperious in competing offlines and made a decisive defensive gesture. With his team leading 12-6, Lynagh lost the ball in his own 40. Guscott picked it up and made the overlap for Andrew. With the ball in his hands, the England fly-half is sailing dangerously into the 22. For a brief moment, the heart of the entire southern nation stopped beating. But suddenly, returning from over the hills and far away at full speed, John Eales administered a tackle from behind that stopped him dead in his tracks. Nothing would come of the offensive. Only a handful of minutes later, Derek Bevan blew the whistle for the end of the game. At the age of 21, the young Australian giant was bringing the world to its feet for the first time.

In 1992, following the success of the previous World Cup, the southern hemisphere resuscitated the Super 6, the forerunner of today's Super Rugby, in which two Australian provinces, three New Zealand provinces and the Fiji national team are competing. Eales' Queensland Reds won the competition, giving him his first major trophy with his province. Unfortunately, shortly afterwards, during the autumn tour, the lock suffers a serious shoulder injury against Llanelli.

After a full year away from the field, John dispelled any fears about his ability to resume playing at the highest level. With the Reds, he won the 1994 Super 10, a Super 6 made up of three South African teams and an additional New Zealand team. He also reappeared in green and gold. With his confidence restored and sharper than ever, he was ready to defend his crown at the next World Cup.

It was around this time that another quality of the prodigy player gradually emerged. Reds coach John Connolly noticed Eales' extraordinary coordination of movement while observing him play cricket. The 45-metre drop-goal that Eales scored for his club Brothers shortly afterwards convinced his coach to give him the challenging role of goalscorer.

With the national team, he also tried his hand at penalty shots at goals, with success. During the World Cup, Michael Lynagh did not feature against Romania. The Wallabies initially relied on the kicks of Matt

Burke. But after Australia's third try, the audience was surprised to see Eales position the ball on the tee. The second row successfully converted off-centre. He just scored his first points with his foot in an international match. He would go on to convert the next three tries with just as much fortune.

These performances were somewhat overshadowed by Australia's spiritless results. Although Eales put in some good performances, he could only watch as his team sank. In the quarter-final, England's Rob Andrew decided the fate of the Wallabies with a last-minute drop-goal. Final score: 25-22. The Australians returned home absolutely gutted. The team had reached the end of its tether. What's more, some of them didn't quite seem to be up to the task during the tournament. Insistent rumours suggest that the prospect of lucrative revenues, brought about by the arrival of professionalism, had turned heads.

Although 1995 did not reach the heights expected for the national team, John Eales enjoyed another Super 10 triumph. The man who became known as 'Ealesy', or 'Mister Cool', once again took the Provincial Championship with the Reds shortly before the World Cup. The Queensland franchise would have to wait until 2011 to win this competition again.

Since his debut for the green and gold in 1991, Ealesy has continued to evolve, improve and strengthen. His level of skills had risen considerably, making him indisputable for the Wallabies. His perception of the game had become highly relevant. Combining speed and natural ability, John often popped up in the three-quarters line at the right time. As his muscularity developed, his power push in the scrum became more dynamic. His volume in defence was becoming more and more impressive. Driven by a pragmatic attitude and a characteristic unwavering phlegm, he successfully commanded the defensive organisation of his teams. With an eye on modern rugby, Mister Cool valued preparation, communication and reflection. For him, these are decisive factors in modern rugby, which he embodied to perfection.

He may surprise and surprise even more on the pitch, but it is in the intimacy of the dressing room that he unites the group around him. Unaffected by pressure, positive even at the worst of times, his serenity was the key to his leadership. He knew perfectly how to channel the energies of his teams while nourishing them with his reflection and intelligence.

It was, therefore, not surprising, or even logical to see Ealesy take on the role of captain of the Wallabies in 1996. The charismatic Michael Lynagh had just bowed out, and a strong man was needed to lead the team to a major event: the first Tri-Nations in history.

The first match under the captaincy of John Eales turned into a fiasco. Australia was swept aside 43-6 in Wellington. The rout became the biggest points difference defeat ever recorded by the national team.

The team managed to manage to rise from the ashes the following week, mainly by rallying around their captain. South Africa was beaten by 21 points to 16 in Sydney. "Seeing the team pull together and beat the South Africans, the then reigning world champions and unbeaten in their last 15 matches, is one of my fondest rugby memories," said Eales after his retirement.

The last two matches ended in respectable defeats: 25-32 to New Zealand and 25-19 to the Springboks. Despite the tough start, coach Greg Smith reaffirmed renewed confidence in his captain, saying that "Eales is the right man for the job."

Mister Cool's boot, which was almost forgotten, came back to the fore in the following years. John became the highest-scoring Wallaby in 1997, with 59 points. In 1998, he became the eighth Australian to exceed 100 points for his country. Finally, against Fiji, he equals Matt Burke's national record of 9 conversions in a single match.

Also, in 1998, the Bledisloe Cup returned to the Wallabies. It is the third time Ealesy has raised the trophy. Unfortunately, another serious shoulder injury kept him out of action for much of 1999, denying him the chance to win the trophy again. Despite the tight timing, he recovered in time to play in his third World Cup.

Despite the return of the charismatic lock, the Australian public had serious doubts about their team's chances of winning the Webb Ellis Cup for a second time. The emblematic captain, in his own distinctive style, played down these fears before the competition: "Most people in Australia think we're not in the best shape. But they are also confident in our abilities."

The 1999 Wallaby vintage was a perfect reflection of its captain. Sober, committed and terribly effective. Without impressing too much, the team's pragmatism shined through. First, they beat the Romanians 57-9 in Belfast. They then avoided the Irish trap, beating the Greens 23-3 at Lansdowne Road. In the final group match, a 55-19 win over the United States, the team conceded its only try of the competition. Yes, the only try!

In the quarter-final, Australia dominated Wales 24-9, then met their old rival South Africa in the semi-final. In a locked match, all the points were scored by kicks. The southern gunners took the lead to give their nation a 27-21 victory.

The final took place on 6th November. The Wallabies were facing the unpredictable French team, who had surprisingly beaten the All Blacks the week before. Les Bleus were unable to find a breakthrough and kept coming up, powerless, against a wall. Matt Burke kicked 7 penalties before Ben Tune broke through the blue defence in the 66th minute. Owen Finnegan followed suit in the dying moments to make it 35-12.

It was at the end of this competition, mastered from start to finish, that John Eales was admitted to the intimate club of players who have won two World Cups. The photo of the Queen of England, as a frail, benevolent grandmother, presenting the Webb Ellis trophy to this colossus in deference to her will be seen all around the world.

After his triumphant return home, Ealesy was honoured as a Member of the Order of Australia for his services to the community and to rugby.

His career, whether with his club or his franchise, has not brought him a title since 1995, and unfortunately, it will not do so again. In a tough, hard-fought Southern Provinces Championship, the Reds had been performing in fits and starts since 1996.

John Eales's international career, nevertheless, would end with a series of highlights. The opening match of the 2000 Tri-Nations, lost to New Zealand, was a match of incredible scenario, described as the match of the century. Three weeks later, the Wallabies were travelling to Wellington with a vengeance and determined to retain the Bledisloe Cup.

The match got off to a perfect start. After just three minutes, following a scrum, Dan Herbert pulled a grigri from his bag of tricks and broke through the defence. He then played perfectly a two-to-one advantage that sent Stirling Mortlock over for a try.

On 17 minutes, after a series of penetrations, Joe Roff raced over to double the lead. But in the action that followed the throw-in, Blacks number 8 Cribb dished out a perfectly weighted kick ahead to Cullen. The fullback's speed made all the difference. The same Cullen repeated the trick in the 23rd minute on a direct attack.

After an offline on Australia's 30-metre line, New Zealand unleashed a simply magnificent set play. Merthens linked around with a block of three forwards positioned in the line before initiating a double scissors between Lomu and Umaga. The latter ripped a hole in the stunned opposition defence before opening off to Cullen, who just had to flatten the ball. If you thought the All Blacks were out, they were only asleep.

From then on, the defences tightened up, and the goalscorers took over on both sides. 20-18 to New Zealand at half-time.

Despite the frenetic pace of the match, both in attack and defence, the score did not change until the 61st minute. Merthens gave his side some breathing space with a penalty kick, but Mortlock hit back immediately. 23 to 21. The Kiwis then took control of the match, and the score stood still once again.

In the 84th minute, Australia wasted no time in trying to play away. Joe Roff was tackled on the opposing 22 metres. In the ensuing contest, Craig Dowd drove into the loose scrum from the side. Referee Jonathan Kaplan whistled a penalty against the New Zealand prop.

Eales immediately pointed to the referee's posts and then looked around for Stirling Mortlock, his regular scorer. But Mortlock had just gone off injured. The Australian captain had seemingly missed the detail. He would have to do the job himself.

Although he used to be the primary scorer in 1997 and 1998, he had since taken a back seat to Matt Burke and Stirling Mortlock. Never mind, he was the man best placed to replace them. He picked up the tee and set the ball up on the 22-metre line, 15 metres from the touchline. Ealesy took two steps back. After a quick concentration, he kicked the ball easily between the posts. The most distinguished of captains just gave his team another Bledisloe Cup, but also the first Tri-Nations in its history.

In a television interview, the main driver recalled the moment in great detail: "We got the penalty. I thought: "This is fantastic, where's Stirling? I looked around, and he wasn't there! Jérémie Paul came up to me and said, "Stirling is out. It's up to you now!" Suddenly, I went from excitement to anxiety. But as a player, it's a moment you've trained for. It's a horrible type of penalty, 15 metres from the line. As a scorer, people expect you to take it. But it was off-centre enough for me to miss it. I'm really very happy to have passed it. I think my life and the memory I've left would have been different if I'd missed that kick."

The Australian giant announced shortly afterwards that he would end his career at the end of the 2001 Tri-Nations. In the meantime, he won the series against the British and Irish Lions for the first time in the Wallabies' history.

John Eales' career came to an end with one last battle with his favourite opponents, the New Zealanders. Leading 19-6 at half-time, Australia thought they were safe. But they were taken by surprise when the All Blacks woke up with a bang, scoring two tries through Alatini and Howlett. They turned the tide and took the lead. In the 66th minute, the Kiwis were leading 26-19. Andrew Walker reduced the deficit with a penalty kick. A terrible battle ensued. The Australians settled in the All Blacks' 22. The defence folded but held firm for almost a quarter of an hour until Kefu, with all his power, managed to break through the line of defence to flatten the ball between the posts.

In his own backyard at Sydney's Australia Stadium, John Eales, who had already become a living legend, enjoyed the send-off he deserved, in keeping with his career. This victory meant that he could retire with a bang by winning a final award, his second Tri-Nations.

When quizzed by journalists, Ealesy firmly closed the door on the possibility of extending his career. "When you've played at the top level, your mind stays at that level. To continue would mean that my mind would be cashing cheques that my body couldn't pay". An eternal philosopher, he concluded with a line once uttered by a former Wallaby, Andrew Slack: "You have to like what you do, not what you've done. That resonates with how I feel right now". Magnificent outing.

Following the end of his career at the age of 31, John Eales was showered with honorary awards. Since 2001, the title of Australian Player of the Year has been known as the John Eales Medal. He was named Queenslander of the Year in 2002, then inducted into a number of Halls of Fame over the following years: Australian Sports, IRB, Wallaby...

In a 12-year career at the highest level, he won 3 Provincial Championship titles, 6 Bledisloe Cups, 2 Tri-Nations and, most impressively, 2 World

Cups. He wore the Wallabies jersey 86 times, each time as a regular. He set the first Australian team captaincy record (since beaten by George Gregan) with 55 caps. Ealesy's feet took him to another peak: with 173 points scored for his country and 402 for the Queensland Reds, he is the highest-scoring forward in the history of rugby. And that record is not about to fall...

Numbers aside, John Eales left his mark on the world of Rugger with his incredible versatility, remarkable speed and exceptional skill. Dominant in attack and resilient in defence, he brought to his teams his sense of play and organisation. Driven by remarkable modesty and maintaining a perfect mental balance even under the most terrible pressure, he had the ability to unite people around these virtues. He left his mark on the teams to which he belonged. Flourishing in Australia but respected the world over, he is one of the greatest examples of world rugby.

Legend has it that he has another nickname, 'Nobody', derived from the adage *Nobody is perfect*. In 2007, he amusedly explained the origin of this nickname: "Nobody's ever called me that! In the mid-1990s, during the Wallabies' end-of-year tour, we decided to give each other little presents. Mitch Hardy gave me a book whose main character was called Mister Perfect. Campo (Campese), whose last tour it was, exclaimed: "That's ridiculous, nobody's perfect!". A member of the team later recounted this to the press. From misinterpretation to misreading, it eventually became: "That's what his teammates call him".

That's how the legend came to be, and wrongly so, because it's certain that no one would have risked saying that this guy was a nobody.

6

2009: The Bastareaud case

Starting with the lie of a player who was no longer an adolescent but not quite an adult, the Bastareaud affair became a scandal. The controversy went beyond rugby and had repercussions even in French and New Zealand politics.

The French national team's 2009 summer tour was off to a flying start. With the 'Dark Destroyer' Thierry Dusautoir in the captain's chair and the two Toulouse rockets Clerc and Heymans on the wings, the French won their first test. They beat the All Blacks 27-22 at Carisbrooke Stadium in Dunedin.

Marc Lièvremont, the French head coach, decided that day to field Mathieu Bastareaud as centre. Bastareaud, who trained at Rugby Créteil-Choisy and then played for Massy before joining Stade Français, has made a dazzling start to his career. A real destroyer of defences and blessed with a heavyweight physique, he came to the attention of Bernard Laporte in 2007. At the time, he played for Massy in Fédérale 1 (third rank French level). Having never played a match in professional competition and aged just 18, he was selected for Les Bleus' summer tour of New Zealand. Unfortunately, a knee injury forced him to withdraw.

After becoming a regular at Stade Français, Marc Lièvremont called him up for the 2009 6 Nations Championship. He made up for Mermoz's injury against Wales. His performance was remarkable, and he retained his first-choice place against England two weeks later. Then, on the final day of the tournament, he replaced Fritz in the 60th minute with a notable entrance. It was, therefore, only natural that he should be included in the squad selected for the summer tour in the southern hemisphere.

After their victory in Dunedin, France travelled to Wellington for a second test against the All Blacks. Les Bleus were beaten 14-10 in what can only be described as a decent defeat. Bastareaud did not play in the match, giving way to Mermoz. Following the two matches in Kiwi country, the French team packed up and headed for Australia, where another test awaited them.

When Mathieu Bastareaud stepped off the plane in Sydney, his face looked strangely swollen. Then, immediately afterwards, the staff of the French national team announced that they would be holding a press conference at their hotel on the same day.

Facing an audience of impatient journalists, Jo Maso announced some astonishing news. On the night of 20th-21st June, Mathieu Bastareaud was out in Wellington when he was mugged. "Four or five of them came at him," said the French manager. As for his condition: "He is suffering from a fairly serious facial trauma. He will undergo tests tomorrow morning to check that he is not suffering from a more serious bone injury," declared Jean-Philippe Hager, the French national team doctor.

Details of the incident were also provided. The player was said to have been attacked after getting out – alone – of the taxi that took him back to the Holiday Inn in Wellington. After being assaulted, he reportedly woke up the team doctor to receive first aid. The staff also said that no complaint had been lodged but that the incident had been reported to the New Zealand Rugby Union. Finally, the misfield back will cut short the tour and return to France early.

The exposure of the incident caused a stir in the press and particularly shocked New Zealanders. What's more, the country was due to host the next World Cup in 2011. The Prime Minister, John Key, had to make a public statement to ensure that the event would take place in total safety for everyone, players and fans alike.

On Monday, 22nd June, while the New Zealand Rugby Association strongly condemned the incident, the Wellington police announced that an investigation had been opened. They questioned Mathieu Bastareaud by telephone. Mathieu then boarded a plane for Paris the same day. On his return home, he issued a press release via his club, Stade Français, to express his "astonishment" at "the extent of the media coverage of this attack, from which he had recovered".

For the next two days, rugby tried to get back into the swing of things. The French team ignored the media hype and remained concentrated on the upcoming match against Australia. Meanwhile, the Wellington police were under pressure and working hard. And it wasn't long before the results of the investigation were revealed.

On the 25th, the New Zealand police disclosed the findings of their investigations, which were immediately relayed by the national press.

Examination of the CCTV recordings made it possible to establish a chronology of events. To everyone's astonishment, we find that Mathieu Bastareaud was in no way attacked outside the hotel, as he had claimed. Nor, according to him, was he alone.

According to the enquiry, Bastareaud, accompanied by two other players and two young women, arrived at the Holiday Inn in two taxis at precisely 5.22 am. The recordings revealed no aggression of any kind. It will be revealed later that the other two men were Montpellier players Ouedraogo and Picamoles.

Analysis of the magnetic room key clearly showed that Mathieu Bastareaud did not return to his room until around 5.50 am, just under half an hour later. Wellington Police boss Pete Cowan closed the enquiry with these words: "All I can tell you is that he was not assaulted outside his hotel by four or five thugs. From my point of view, the case is closed."

A few hours later, the young Parisian centre three-quarter, caught in the middle and overwhelmed by his lie, wrote an official statement on the Stade Français website: "On Saturday night, I went back to the hotel after drinking too much. I fell in my room, hit the bedside table and cut my cheekbone. I felt ashamed, I panicked, and I thought I was going to get kicked out of the French team". He then went on to apologise to the whole world: New Zealand, his club, his national team, his friends, fans of all stripes, etc…

Betrayed and dismayed, Jo Maso, in turn, publicly apologised before saying wearily: "For our part, there was no desire to hide anything. We defended our player. Unfortunately, he lied to everyone. I'm deeply hurt." He was immediately followed by Pierre Camou, President of the FFR, who also indicated that he had already referred the matter to the federation's disciplinary committee. The consequences of the lie were taking on ever greater proportions.

In New Zealand, a country still reeling from the Rainbow Warrior affair, journalists and politicians were castigating the liar Bastareaud. The French people were also getting it in their necks. The Mayor of Wellington publicly expressed her indignation, while the press did not hesitate to refer to the events as the *Rainbow Warrior of rugby*. Prime Minister François Fillon also had no choice but to issue a letter of apology to the whole of New Zealand.

Now that the shock was over, public opinion wanted the truth to come out. Did Mathieu Bastareaud really injure himself, as he claimed? Some journalists suggested that he had an altercation with Ouedraogo and/or Picamoles on the way back to the Holiday Inn that night. And the presence of the two young women could have been the reason. Jo Maso denied this without any real conviction: "I've had no indication that this was the case."

Other members of staff, including the team doctor, soberly doubted the version put forward by the young player: "He was in shock but didn't look drunk."

The player himself cut short the controversy in the most dramatic way possible. Harassed by the press, along with his family, and shamed for having cast aspersions on those around him and his team-mates, Mathieu Bastareaud attempted suicide in the final days of June. "I don't know if I really wanted to die, but the only certainty I have is that I wanted to inflict a lot of suffering on myself because I thought I deserved it," he confessed a few years later.

It was Max Guazzini, the president of his club, who informed AFP (French Press Association) that Bastareaud had been hospitalised for "serious psychological problems", adding: "He's devastated, he needs to be left alone." The fatherly Guazzini would be the first to put the lid on the situation: "Mathieu's reaction was childish. He was overwhelmed by his lie. He didn't press charges, so there was no perjury. As far as I'm concerned, the incident is over."

Marc Lièvremont was not blaming his player either. He would still have every chance of being selected if his level of play proved worthy of that of an international.

Supported and surrounded by his family and Stade Français team-mates, Mathieu Bastareaud gradually returned to the pitch after his convalescence. "We got him back totally shattered, in absolute ruin. The demons were there for a long time. But with strength and self-sacrifice, he got back on his feet," testified his team-mate Mathieu Blin. On 14th August, he was included in the 22-man squad for his club's match against RC Toulon. Then, on 19th September, a few days before he was due to appear before the Disciplinary Committee, he marked his comeback by scoring his first try of the season against Bourgoin.

On 28th September, the FFR peers sanction Bastareaud with a 3-month suspension. The sanction would be immediately commuted to 18 hours of community service. Finally, at the end of October, just as he was about to carry out his first community service, the young and talented rugby player threw a definitive veil over this lie too big for him by apologising once again – and for the last time – publicly.

In a sign of a new-found confidence, Marc Lièvremont fielded him in the 2010 6 Nations Championship. Mathieu Bastareaud played an active role in that year's Grand Slam, scoring two tries in four games as a regular.

To this day, it has still not been revealed what happened between 5.20 am and 5.50 am on the morning of 21st June. Whenever he is asked, Mathieu Bastareaud invariably repeats the same story: he injured himself. Hypothetically, with the help of revelations from a player or member of staff who took part in the 2009 tour, the story of this incident may well change…

7

1997: Welcome to the Wild South

Opening the slap box was customary in the high-level rugby of yesteryear. And the presence of television cameras in no way diminished the generosity of the exchanges. Following the same habits, the feelings would happily run lower over a few drinks during the post-match reception. However, some of the grudge-holder players broke with tradition, and even though few drinks had been served, they continued to have a scrap during the third half.

On 14th September 1997, reigning European champions CA Brive hosted Pontypridd RFC. At the time, Brive's Parc Municipal des Sports was a real cauldron, white-hot with supporters euphoric about the club's recent successes. In the corridor, the Brive forwards were overplaying their roles, exchanging punches with each other and grossly provoking the Welshmen lined up next to them. The Welsh, unimpressed, kept their composure but were ready to draw. According to fly-half Neil Jenkins: 'If they started something, we were prepared to finish it'. Who said the Ponty boys are going to keep a low profile?

If they had been defeated the previous week at home to Bath, it was only because of a dubious try by Mike Catt. And having been specially prepared for the event by their coach, Eddie Jones, they came to challenge the European champions in their own garden without any hang-ups. 'Our team manager Eddie Jones had talked a lot about the need to show some of the old Ponty fire and to get in among the French', recalls Martyn Williams.

Provocative, the Australian coach would also send a warning to Brive by declaring: 'We've got the bottle for it. We don't get intimidated easily, which is what French sides like to do. They don't give you apples; they give you the swede!'

Although Pontypridd were not the reigning European champions, the fact remains that the Welsh were not a second-rate team. They proved it by holding Brive a candle. In the first half, around the 24th minute, Dale McIntosh – 'Chief' to his friends – a Welsh international of New Zealand origin, tackled Philippe Carbonneau slightly late on. Lionel Mallier played the role of vigilante and had a field day with the Welsh number 8. The former received a red card and left the field with a bloodied eyebrow. The same punishment was meted out to the second, who left the pitch taunting and inveighing against the home team's fans.

The visitors led until a few minutes from the end. But after a penetrating maul, Patrick Lubungu scored a power try, which was questionable. The match concluded with a narrow score of 32-31. Ponty left the pitch bitterly resentful of the unduly awarded points and the incessant provocations from Brive. 'There was a lot of tug-of-war, a lot of things that the cameras didn't catch,' John explained later,' They knew how to hit you underhand. They'd pinch you, slash you, hit your ankles or your fingers; they wanted a reaction.'

Despite a tumultuous afternoon, all these skirmishes were thought to remain facts of the game. Following the post-match reception, the Coujoux (Brive players's nickname) left the stadium and celebrated the victory in style. Clearly not holding a grudge, they invited their opponents of the day to join them. 'I remember them saying to us: 'Come down, there's a bar called Le Toulzac in town',' says Jenkins. 'In retrospect, we should have stayed away.'

The Brivists were the first to reach the bar, run by two former CAB players: the late Jean-Marie Soubira and Bruno Marty.

In the evening, a dozen or so home team players, including Lamaison, Carbonneau, Venditti and Casadéï, surrounded by their fans, were celebrating the victory when they saw their Welsh counterparts investing the place. As Pontypridd would not be returning home until the following day, they decided to pay their respects to the invitation made a few hours earlier. 'When we arrived all together, I think they wondered what was going on. That's what we tended to do. If we went, we all went,' explains Jenkins.

With the guests arriving, the atmosphere in the Toulzac cooled down a little, but the evening went on all the same. McIntosh, excited and visibly drunk, took a seat and set his eyes on a bottle of white wine. Before long, the first 'fuck Carbonneau!' were heard. Three Welshmen seem particularly angry with the French scrum-half: number 8 Dale McIntosh, hooker Phil John and the famous fly-half Neil Jenkins. To them, the

Frenchman's repeated foul games had tipped the match irregularly in Brive's favour.

The atmosphere was getting heavier and heavier. You could feel the electricity in the air. Philippe Carbonneau, far to be intimidated, did not leave the venue. On the contrary, he approached the Welsh group after being invited. But after a few words, the situation ignited like wildfire. "All of a sudden, all hell broke loose, and the bar became like a scene in a Wild West movie with bottles and chairs flying everywhere', adds the Welsh international fly-half.

What could have set things off so suddenly? Depending on who you ask, the story varies. For Martyn Williams, whose words were confirmed by John: 'Later, I found out that Carbonneau and Phil John were the two involved at the start of it. Phil thought Carbonneau was winding him up, so there was a bit of aggro between them. That was sort of brought under control after a bit, and we all decided it was best to leave. But then, as we were leaving, a bottle was thrown at us from where the Brive players were standing, and it caught Jason on the head. That was it. That was the signal for all hell to break loose.'

On the French side, David Venditti states that it was the Ponty Men who started the fray: 'I was talking to Neil Jenkins when I saw that McIntosh and Phil John were threatening Carbonneau. None of the 'local' witnesses will mention a bottle being thrown, but they will all remember seeing McIntosh open the hostilities with a masterful punch to the face of Carbonneau.'

The truth about how the fuse was lit undoubtedly lies somewhere between these two different accounts. But the fact remains that, now that the free-for-all was open, everyone's rushing in!

The furious Welsh immediately pounced on Carbonneau, determined to give him a hard time. Lamaison and Mallier tried to intervene, but they were quickly put out by the enraged opponents. Casadei, Travers, and Venditti also threw themselves headlong into the hustle and bustle, which was extremely violent, and tried to stand their ground.

Panic-stricken customers and players' families are fussing all around. Some took part in the battle, others tried to get out of the bar, while another group took refuge upstairs in the bosses' office. The bosses, unable to control such an outburst of brutality, attempted to get Carbonneau to safety. 'I tried to pull Philippe behind the counter [...], but we took a huge beating. At one point, you start wondering how you're going to get out of it,' recalls Bruno Marty.'

Time stood still for a few more moments of violent exchanges before the fury subsided. The audience finally managed to push the Ponty men back outside the Toulzac. Then the roller shutter came down, like a drawbridge ensuring the safety of the Brivists entrenched in the premises.

Everyone could catch their breath. The bistro was totally devastated. The furniture was upside down, shattered and mixed with broken glass on a floor stained with blood. The people who had taken refuge upstairs slowly reappeared and, still in shock, began to clean up the damage.

As humanity slowly regained the upper hand in a ravaged Toulzac, it was decided to reopen the metal gate, no doubt to ventilate the atmosphere. A group of Welshmen, led by a visibly not quite sated Martyn Williams, stepped into the breach and burst back into the bar!

With their fists out, they once again started dealing with anyone who got in their way. But this time, they had to contend with Congolese colossus

Patrick Lubungu. Turned into Bud Spencer, he cooled the Welsh ardour with a series of monstrous blasts.

At the same moment, the police arrived at the site. Taken aback by this unusual, almost unrealistic scene, they hesitated for a moment. Didier Casadeï couldn't take it anymore, so he grabbed the baton from one of them and jumped back into the fray. Sabering like a hussar, he would finally be able to restore calm to the establishment. 'I was lucky, I was able to club the guys in the face', he said simply afterwards.

The general brawl would leave some physical after-effects in the Brivist ranks: Fractured noses for Lamaison and Carbonneau and a dislocated finger for Venditti, who apparently also received treatment for a bite wound. While some were heading to the hospital to support the injured, others were going to the police station to lodge a complaint. The episode was too violent to remain with the *status quo*.

The visitors returned to their hotel. Martyn Williams was stitched up by team doctor Dave Pemberton. He then rejoined his teammates, who had spontaneously gathered to discuss the evening's events. Then they all went to bed, convinced that the incident would end there.

The courts would take the first step in the final outcome. The very next morning, six players were arrested at their hotel and taken, handcuffed, into police custody. They were McIntosh, John, Barnard, Williams and the Lewis brothers.

The last three were quickly released, while Josh McIntosh, Andrew Barnard and 'Ghurka' Phil John would be invited to spend the following night in solitary confinement for the purposes of the investigation. Indicted, they would be banned from the Corrèze département for several years. At the end of the inquiry, they were convicted for the violence perpetrated on the rugby field. As for the real street fight that took place at Taulzac, the French justice authorities attempted to establish, without any real success, who was responsible for what. The Welsh would not answer subsequent summonses, and the case would die on its own.

Neil Jenkins saw the dropping of the charges as entirely legitimate, as he believes that the Brive were used to ambushing their opponents during the third half: 'We only learned afterwards that what usually happened was that they invited teams to come over and ended up fighting with them.'

In France, voices were being raised following this wild evening. Some were calling for Pontypridd to be excluded from the European Cup. Others urged the Brive men not to play the return match in Wales. The ERC also seized on the matter. Despite strong protests from CAB chairman Patrick Sébastien, both clubs would be fined the same amount: £30,000 each.

During the two weeks between the first and second legs, the Pontypridd club opened its doors wide to the press. In a communication campaign led by Jeff Jones, the club's vice-chairman, the Welsh side emphasised that 'never was an opposition kicker whistled at' and that 'the Sardis Road stadium is a place where you can take your children and they won't learn bad manners'. He also insists that Pontypridd's nickname, The Family Club, 'speaks for itself'.

The Brivists seem less inclined to appeasement. Patrick Sébastien banned his supporters from travelling to Wales. He also stated that he intended to travel to Sardis Road, escorted by his bodyguards.

The return match, which took place on 27th September, would be an opportunity for everyone to put this ugly story behind them. There would be no foul play, no bad spirit, no whistles or jeers from the stands. Everyone was satisfied and happy with the draw, 29-29. As a symbol, Christophe Lamaison, his face still bruised, scored 24 points for his team that day.

At the final whistle, a few shy handshakes were exchanged. The day's opponents shared the common shower rooms, and then the Brive players headed straight for Cardiff airport.

There were still a number of unanswered questions: were the Pontypridd players determined to do battle on the night of the brawl? Did Brivists deliberately set a trap for their opponents by inviting them to the Taulzac? And above all, should Philippe Carbonneau be considered the victim or the aggressor?

For Casadeï, the action was premeditated: 'They wanted to take Philippe Carbonneau on'. Neil Jenkins, on the other hand, said the exact opposite afterwards: 'We'd been invited [...] I'd come with my wife. When we went in, everything was calm [...] I even had a chat with some of the Brive players. There was no sign of what happened next.'

Philippe Carbonneau, who was the catalyst and may well have provoked this outburst of violence, has never spoken on the topic since the incident

8

Nightmare at Kamp Staaldraad

Commando camps were originally created to teach elite troops how to survive in hostile environments. They can also be used, in milder versions, to prepare sports teams for major events. The South Africans used them to prepare for the 2003 World Cup. Their internship in a police training camp, or rather re-education camp, in September 2003 was by no means a light touch and had disastrous sporting and human consequences.

When former lock or back row forward Rudolf Straeuli, the 1995 World Cup champion, was appointed Springboks coach in 2002, he inherited a team that was falling into disarray. The level of the team was far removed from that which had been at the forefront of the oval planet just a few years earlier.

The South Africans finished in last position in the 2002 Tri-Nations, with just one victory. They then lost 30-10 in France in November before being thrashed 52-3 by England. In 2003, as the World Cup was approaching, their results were desperately not taking off. They once again finished at the bottom of the Tri-Nations with just one win to their name.

Straeuli, powerless to create the cohesion his team sorely lacked, decided to strike hard. His aim was to shock the national team. Shortly after announcing the squad for the World Cup, he invited his players to a preparatory training camp. The program had been concocted by his deputies and would be supervised by former members of the elite police force.

The gathering was to be held at a police camp near Thabazimbi in the South African bush. The Springboks reached the venue by bus. When they arrived near the barracks that were to house them, the bus stopped. Everyone got off, and after a brief welcome, they were asked to undress and then crawl down a gravel path to the barracks.

Although taken aback, they complied with this unconventional request and reached the barracks on their elbows. Their instructors, who were about to become executioners, then ordered them to get dressed, undress again and return to the bus in the same way they came from it. As soon as the first protests were heard, a burst of automatic weapons was fired into the air. Here was a foreshadowing of what was to come for the Springbok group.

The rules were then laid down. From now on, each player would be given a number and would have to answer "Yes" or "Sir "every time an instructor spoke to him. Taking organization a step further, some players were forced to tear up the identity papers and photos they had brought with them, as well as smashing their mobile phones. And the most reluctant were once again threatened with weapons.

Rudolf Straeuli admitted later that the aim of the training camp was to destroy any individualistic appetite and to ensure that each individual was devoted body and soul to the Springbok group. Joe Van Niekerk, 22 at the time and regarded as one of South Africa's great hopefuls, only recently confided about his time at Kamp Staaldraad: "They wanted to break us down, humiliate us, terrify us. I even lost two kilos in three days."

The gruelling physical exercises, such as carrying tyres, timbers or heavy bags decorated with the colours of England or New Zealand, followed one another.

The harassing sessions were interspersed with practices bordering on torture, both mental and physical, seeking to go even further in the degradation of each individual.

One hardship was invariably cited by all the Springboks who took part in this camp: for hours on end, they had to crawl through narrow trenches and galleries, regularly doused with ice-cold water, with the English anthem or the New Zealand haka played out loudly from the loudspeakers.

John Smit also remains marked by the nights he spent in the desert. "We were starving. The guards lit a fire, opened a box with live chickens and said to us: "Here's your supper! You've got a fire; do what you want!". Van Niekerk also describes his horror at this episode: "I grew up in Johannesburg. I'm a city boy, and I've never killed a chicken in my life. What's more, the soldiers refused to give us a knife. We had to kill the chickens with our own hands. I think some of the players bled them using their teeth. What a nightmare!".

After they ate, they all had to spend the rest of the night in the South African bush. Their instructors, not to say executioners, would spend the night tormenting their sleep, unexpectedly firing bursts of automatic weapons into the air.

The most memorable episode, in which everyone felt humiliated and lower than dirt, was the one in the lake. Early in the morning, the 30 players are obliged to strip completely naked and then plunge into a pond of terribly cold, muddy water. While some were forming a circle, holding each other by the shoulders, others had to dive underwater to inflate rugby balls. When the captain at the time, Korne Krige, got bold and tried to reach the shore, he was dissuaded by two shots fired in the direction of the ground.

After three days of bullying, forced nudity and all kinds of humiliation, everyone was sent home, but not before swearing an oath never to reveal the exact content of the preparatory course.

However, like post-traumatic shock, such taunts were beginning to haunt some of the participants. "If I were the team leader, I would never have agreed to put my teammates at such risk. A commando course is a way of preparing like any other, but they went too far," Van Niekerk later confides.

The matter was put to rest, at least for a while. Shortly afterwards, the South Africans flew to Australia. The World Cup opened on 10th October, and the Springboks took on Uruguay on 11th October. They had a satisfactory group phase, easily overcoming a number of opponents, but still lost 25-6 to eventual champions England.

In the quarter-final, the Rainbow Nation's players were up against an opponent they knew well: New Zealand. Defeated 29-9 in a match in which they struggled to make an impact, Straeuli's men packed up and headed home. The electroshock did not come, and the poor performances of recent years were confirmed.

A few days after the Boks were eliminated, the scandal broke. In mid-November, the circumstances surrounding the stay at Kamp Staaldraad were leaked to the newspapers. A photo appears in many of the Anglo-Saxon media, showing the players naked in the famous pool of icy water, with, to use a widely-used phrase, "only rugby balls to hide their dignity".

We won't have to look very hard before we uncover the whistleblower. It's Dale McDermott, the team's video analyst. To relieve himself of this heavy burden that was weighing too heavily on him or for financial gain, he decided to make this photo publicly available.

At the same time, two players who wished to remain anonymous were also making revelations about what they endured during those three days. Then a third, also anonymous, member of the team told English newspaper *The Guardian*: "There have been a few incidents that I find shocking, but I'll tell you about them when Straeuli will have been fired. If any of us speak out, we'll be in trouble and will certainly have to look for a club in France or elsewhere."

As public outrage grew in South Africa, the federation denied any involvement in the organisation of the camp. And it assured Straeuli and his staff of its support. SARU maintains that the coach took part in the camp but only as an observer. According to Gideon Sam, one of the team's managers, "the lads were roughed up, but that's what's involved in preparing for a battle".

The affair quickly spread beyond the sporting aspect. Some senior army officers were speaking out publicly. They claimed that no army in the world would allow its men to be sent naked for training, as it is so degrading. Sports psychology specialists were also getting involved. For them, individualism was a factor that could tip a match in the right direction. Consequently, trying to break down individuality had been counter-productive for the Springboks. Judging by their performance at the World Cup, the conclusion of this analysis made sense.

We also take a closer look at Adriaan Heijns, Rudolf Straeuli's right-hand man. A former member of the police special forces under apartheid, he was officially the deputy in charge of logistics. In reality, he followed Straueli like a shadow, observing the every move of every member of the group. He also categorically refused to give anyone the players' room numbers when they stayed in a hotel. "He's there to control us", said a member of the 2003 group, speaking anonymously. Heinjs was also responsible for setting up the Kamp Staaldraad program.

At this stage of the scandal, apart from anonymous declarations, players and members of staff were playing it safe, sometimes contradicting each other. Gideon Sam, for example, denied the veracity of the episode involving the icy pond of water, while Krige asserted the opposite a few hours later. As for the presence of firearms in the camp, the same Krige maintained that there were none. The famous Joost Van Der Westhuizen would contradict him shortly afterwards but would play down their use. According to him, the weapons were simply used to wake up the players and get certain exercises underway.

One of the main subjects of indignation, forced nudity during certain exercises, was also subject to various interpretations. Korn Krige maintained that the players removed their clothes because of the unpleasant rubbing they caused. Songezo Nayo claimed that Nike failed to provide adequate clothing for aquatic exercises. But Heinjs' comments were the most memorable, cold and far from politically correct: "When you're naked, all your pretensions vanish. It levels the playing field".

A few days later, questions of racial discrimination rocked a Springbok staff that was more vulnerable than ever. Sports Minister Ngconde Balfour calls Straeuli to account for the removal of several coloured players from the squad (notably Quinton Davids). The official also insisted that the Geo Cronje case be reopened. The lock had been accused of racist remarks the previous summer. The federation cleared him of all charges but still excluded him from the squad.

That was way too much for public opinion in a country where the oval ball is king. Over the last two years, the South African national team had suffered one disappointment after another. First, the heaviest defeat ever at home to New Zealand. Then, the biggest defeats ever were against France, England and Scotland. And finally, a dismal exit at the quarter-final stage of the World Cup. Add to that the latest events, and someone had to pick up the bill.

Straeuli received a summons to present himself to the South African Federation office on 5th December. The reason was explicit: to discuss the coach's future. After receiving the letter, he simply stated: "My contract runs for another two years. If the federation dismisses me, the compensation will be in the region of £300,000".

Rudolf Straeuli finally resigned on 4th December, followed by several of his deputies. According to SARU, "a solution was found that did not harm either party".

However, the epilogue to the Kamp Staaldraad scandal would be dramatic for Dale McDermott, the whistleblower who brought the affair to light. He had to resign from his position at the Council for Scientific and Industrial Research, from which he had been detached to the Springboks. Having become persona non grata in the world of rugby, he turned to second-hand car-seller. He took his own life on 5th January 2005, shot in the head.

Should the ordeals imposed on the Springboks during that preparation camp be considered immoral and degrading? Should they be described as torture? Or was the uproar surrounding these incidents simply a cry of despair from the press and fans of a desperate national team?

For Joe Van Niekerk, evoking these memories remains painful. Brighton Paulse is more nuanced: "I nearly cracked up when we were in the pit. But the rest wasn't so bad". Kriege agrees: "I wouldn't recommend certain parts of the camp. But others were good for the team spirit". Ricardo Laubscher goes even further when he talks about the time spent in the pool of cold water: "It wasn't much different from the ice baths we use for recovery".

The winner takes all. What would have happened if the Boks had won the 2003 World Cup? Would Rudolf Straeuli have been praised for his unorthodox methods? And would this kind of preparation have become the norm in modern rugby?

9

2009: A bloody wink

In order to prevent the transmission of serious viral diseases, rugby authorities have long had a rule about temporary replacements due to bleeding. Many cases of abuse of this rule have been suspected. Simulated or fake bleeding may have been used to simply give certain players a breather. Most of the ambiguous facts have never been officially confirmed, with the exception of the so-called Bloodgate affair. In 2009, Harlequins were caught with their hands in the jam pot.

After two seasons spent battling in the bottom half of the Guinness Premiership, 2008/09 was a completely different story for Harlequins. After finishing 2nd in the regular season of the Championship, they fell in the semi-final stage to London Irish. On the European scene, the Quins disputed the prestigious Heineken Cup. They also put in some very good results. Competing in a pool made up of Ulster, Stade Français and Llanelli Scarlets, they only conceded one defeat at Ravenhill in Ireland. As a result, they booked their ticket for the quarter-final.

The draw was fortunate for Harlequins, who had the advantage of playing this European quarter-final on home soil at Twickenham Stoop Stadium.

However, the match promised to be a hard-fought affair. The Quins had to face Leinster, with its plethora of Irish internationals (who would win the title that season).

On 12th April 2009, two months after the end of the group matches, under a cottony sky, the H Cup was back at the Stoop Stadium. Needless to say, the stakes were high: if the Quins managed to overcome the Irish, they would have the opportunity to play in their first semi-final in this competition. And why not dream of the title?

Dean Richards, the English club's coach, was no stranger to high-stakes matches. A 46-time England international, he played in three World Cups and one European Cup final (losing to Brive in 1997), winning two Championships and three RFU Knockout Cups. He then had a brilliant debut coaching career with Leicester: four consecutive English Championships (1999, 2000, 2001, 2002) and a European double (2001 and 2002). In 2009, he was dreaming of taking the Quins to the summit of Europe.

Richards then concocted a meticulous preparation for his group. And on the day of the quarter-final, he fielded his A-side team. New Zealander Nick Evans started at fly-half. Evans scored a lifesaving drop-goal to secure a 19-17 victory over Stade Français in the group stage.

The game was a rough, hard-fought affair, with both sides failing to score. In the first half, Nick Evans strived to liven up his backline. But England's ferocious offensives were broken by Leinster's rock-solid defence, led by O'Driscoll and D'Arcy. At the break, Leinster went into the changing room with a 6-0 lead, but Contepomi had still managed to kick two penalties.

Shortly after the start of the second half, in the 47th minute, Harlequins lost their playmaker Evans, who went off with a knee injury. Australian Chris Malone substituted, and the onslaught on the Irish home side resumed in earnest. The Quins' persistence finally paid off in the 66th minute. After a long sequence of play inside the opposition 10 metres, fullback Mike Brown pierced the defensive curtain and touched down in the in-goal.

Malone, who also took on the role of goalscorer by replacing Evans, had the opportunity to turn his side's dominance into points. Unfortunately, the conversion went wide. Leinster still led 6-5 at this point in the match.

The Irish regained the initiative and, after a phase of champagne rugby, created a loose scrum inside England's 22. Nothing came of the action, but one Quins remained on the ground: Chris Malone. The second fly-half was struck down by thigh pain and was carried off the field by two attendants.

Dean Richards now had two options available to replace him. On the bench waited the experienced scrum-half Andy Gormarsall and versatile fullback/winger Tom Williams. Strangely enough, the London tactician opted for the second option.

In the 72nd, an umpteenth penalty kick, attempted from 54 metres out by third kicker Browne, failed. Harlequins were sensing that the game was slipping away from them. Then Fortune decided to throw another spanner in the works two minutes later. Williams got up from a ruck with heavy bleeding coming from his mouth. He looked a little groggy and left the pitch, accompanied by the team physio. As he was making his way to the dressing room to be examined, he winked enigmatically at his manager by way of greeting.

With Richard still unable to bring on Gomarsall, Evans hobbled back onto the pitch. Confusion ensued for a few moments. The fourth referee initially refused to let the player onto the pitch. The first referee, the experienced Nigel Owens, then reminded him of a rule: a player cannot return to the pitch after being substituted... unless it is a temporary replacement due to bleeding.

With only two minutes left to play, Leinster conceded a penalty on the halfway line. The Quins chose to go into touch. After a series of rucks on the 22-metre line, Nick Evans found himself in the perfect position to attempt a drop-goal. The Stoop Stadium crowd was pushing like a sixteenth man. The fans were hoping with all their might that Evans would pull off another winning kick, as he had done against Stade Français earlier in the season.

Unfortunately for the English, the drop-goal attempt went to the left of the posts. A few phases of play later, the referee relieved the Irish by blowing his whistle for the end of the match. That was the end of London's hopes. Although they had dominated the game, they were out of the competition.

This match could simply have been added to the list of unusual encounters in the world of Rugger. But the rugby universe soon begins to buzz about this quarter-final.

First of all, many were surprised by the abundant bleeding coming from Williams' mouth following his injury. The images of the Englishman leaving the field, coughing up a river of blood, were indeed quite striking. While it was common for injuries to the scalp or eyebrows to cause impressive haemorrhaging, injuries to the mouth generally bleed very little.

Also, in the corridor leading to the dressing room, the Leinster doctor, who insisted on seeing the wound, was kept away from the injured player by the Quins staff. He returned a few moments later, accompanied by representatives of the ERC, and again asked to be allowed to examine the wound. All were curtly refused, and the door to the first-aid post was slammed in their faces. The match referee, Owens, was informed immediately after the final whistle that Leinster officials suspected a spurious operation. However, after receiving treatment, Tom Williams reappeared with a cut on his lip that was not fake.

Having heard about what had gone on behind the scenes, Irish television got hold of the story and rewatched the videos with attention. The England fly-half was injured when he was out of camera sight. From then on, it was impossible to know how the wound was caused. Once again, the journalists highlighted the extent of the bleeding. But above all, they dwelled on a detail which, given the situation, was fraught with innuendo: why did Williams wink at Richards as he left the pitch? And why was Nick Evans' knee hastily strapped around the 66th minute?

On 17th April, after five days of debates, the Heineken Cup management announced that an investigation would be conducted by the ERC Disciplinary Committee. It was quickly established that Steph Brennan, the club's physiotherapist, bought fake blood capsules in a joke shop on Dean Richards's orders. The deception could no longer be concealed. The enquiry concluded that Richards was the instigator of the cheating. Tom Williams was found guilty of biting into the blood capsule. Although he was certainly the victim of strong pressure from his coach, 'he had the option of refusing at any time', according to the ERC. Finally, Steph Brennan was also caught up in the turmoil, having bought and provided the Quins winger with the equipment needed for the hoax.

A further investigation was ordered the following weeks to establish the role played by Wendy Chapman, the Harlequins doctor. The decision was then reserved.

The sentence was handed down on 20th July. Harlequins and Tom Williams were found guilty of cheating. The club was fined €250,000, while the player was handed a 12-month suspension. Richards, Brennan and Chapman were cleared of all charges.

On 31st July, Williams announced that he would appeal against the decision, and that "all light will be shed on the events". The Quins management, alarmed at the consequences of these revelations, immediately launched an internal enquiry. Richards, seeing that the situation was about to get completely out of hand, resigned on 8th August.

The commission met for an appeal on 17th August. Everyone was hanging on Williams' every word, and he played the repentance card. Steph Brennan bought fake blood capsules at Richards' request and supplied one to the player. He hid it in his sock, waiting for the right opportunity to bite into it. Then, once inside the first-aid post, he asked Doctor Chapman to cut his lip. She refused. He threatened her. Seeing that his threats didn't work, he told her that he would mutilate himself. The doctor relented: "I was afraid that Williams would cause himself irreparable damage. So I agreed to cut his lip with a scalpel".

The next part of the confession concerned the institutional side of the fraud. The player had already indicated that he was put under pressure by his coach to commit the criminal act. Then, after being sanctioned by the Disciplinary Committee at first instance, the club's directors allegedly offered him compensation if he dropped his appeal. The idea was to avoid 'stirring up more mud'. The offer included financial compensation, a contract extension and a job of convenience at the end of his playing career.

This time, the punishment would be much heavier. The fine imposed on Harlequins was increased to €300,000. Dean Richards was suspended from all rugby-related employment for three years. Steph Brennan, the physio, had also been suspended for two years by the IRB. Dr Chapman, who was accused of merely participating in the cover-up, was cleared by the ERC but suspended pending a potential sanction from the Medical Council. As for Tom Williams, his suspension was reduced to 4 months.

Facing the tidal wave caused by the scandal, Charles Jillings, the Harlequins chairman, resigned, taking responsibility for being unable to contain the outbursts of his coach, Richards. However, he tried to clear himself and drag Williams down with him: "We never tried to buy the player's silence. He wanted to take advantage of the situation to extort from us a contract extension at a much higher salary, as well as an exorbitant sum of money to drop his appeal".

Dean Richards made no excuses. He simply justified himself by saying that fake bleeding was commonplace and that the ploy had already been used within the Quins squad (a fact confirmed by Brennan). He also added that Clive Woodward used this type of method to lead the Rose XV to the world title in 2003. He disappeared from the radar during the three years of his suspension before making a comeback in 2012 as manager of Newcastle Falcons.

Brennan, for his part, lost a lot in this affair. Although his sentence, deemed too harsh, was reduced on appeal, he had taken up the position of head physio on the England team when the scandal broke. It is a position he had always dreamed of and one from which he had now been forced to resign. He also lost his position at the Newcastle Sports Clinic before falling back into anonymity for a while. He bounced back in 2012 when he became head physio at Sydney Roosters XII rugby club.

Wendy Chapman caught up in the storm of scandal, left her position as an emergency doctor at Maidstone Hospital. Summoned to report to the medical council, she did not face dismissal but was severely reprimanded by her peers.

The state of mind of the Harlequins squad would be discussed at length by Ugo Monye, a three-quarter who was playing for the team at the time. He wrote at length in an article for The Guardian newspaper: "Our image was severely tarnished. When we said we played for the Quins, people invariably mentioned the affair [...] Many of us agreed, however, that if we were Tom, we too would have bitten into that capsule. But everyone would have dealt with the consequences differently. We didn't blame Tom for telling the truth, but we were puzzled by his ambiguity. He had tried to have it both ways: on the one hand, to have his sanction reduced, and on the other, to pocket the large sum of money promised by the directors for his silence. Tom explained that without recognising it, he had been caught up in the vicious circle of winning at all costs. But I don't think he was simply naive. There was more to it than that. No doubt he wanted to impress Richards".

Could the match referee, Welshman Nigel Owens, also have been involved? He tells the press about the incident, "You can say I'm naive, but it never crossed my mind that something like that could happen. It didn't occur to me to check whether it was fake blood, nor was I qualified to do so. Without any medical background, I wouldn't have gone against a doctor's advice anyway". At a time when players' health is an increasingly important issue, we can't disagree with him.

Tom Williams, the lead actor in this comedy, looked for himself for a while in the wake of the scandal. According to Ugo Monye, "Tom hesitated to end his career. He also tried to find another club, but all the doors were closed at him. After this affair, we found a broken man". He eventually wore the club's colours until 2015, when he became part of the coaching staff at the Quins training centre. He entered the Harlequins 200 Club, having played more than 200 games for his team.

Following the incident, the traumatize squad was taken in hand by Irishman Conor O'Shea. He began by healing his players' souls. His work would pay off in 2012, when the Quins won the English Championship, beating Leicester in the final. That day, Tom Williams scores a try as if to close the book on one of the most stinking scandals in the history of rugby.

10.1

Marc Cécillon: The stainless band leader

Shots rang out. In the face of a stunned crowd, a woman in her fifties collapses, mortally wounded by 357 Magnum bullets. The gunman fell to his knees and shouted, "I love her! Kill me!" The man looked like a colossus. Despite his greying temples, he was athletic, with broad shoulders and a chest as thick as a castle wall. After the astonishment, the men in the audience all jumped on him. About fifteen of them would have to join forces to subdue this force of nature, who, under the combined effect of alcohol and adrenalin, was no longer in control of herself.

Nothing could be done to keep the victim alive. At the beginning of this evening, Marc Cécillon, a former French rugby international, had just taken the life of his wife, Chantal.

Marc Cécillon from Saint-Savin, near Lyon. Born on 30th July 1959, he is the only boy among his siblings. His father, a foreman at car manufacturer Berliet, played rugby, as did his father before him. So, it was only natural that little Marc should embrace the family's passion for the oval ball.

At the age of 7, he joined his local club, Saint-Savin Sportif. And so he fell into the caldron from an early age. This fever would never leave him. He would go on to climb to the very top of the Rugger world, building up an almost divine aura. But as a man of passion, Marc Cécillon would let himself become carried away by the limelight and the adrenalin of top-level sport until it ate him up from the inside out.

When it came to choosing a career path, the young man opted for an apprenticeship in pastry-making. His apprenticeship master, Louis Marchand, was a renowned pastry chef. He trained, among others, the renowned Michelin-starred chef Guy Savoy.

Marchand, renowned for his desserts, was also known in the area for another of his occupations: he was a member of the management team at CS Bourgoin-Jallieu, the region's flagship club.

Louis kept a constant eye on his apprentice's rugby prowess. Marc oozed rugby from every pore of his skin. A humble, discreet and hard-working player, his physical development was impressive. Quickly topping the metre 90 mark and weighing in at 110kg, he shatters defences. Then, when the Saint-Savin Sportif jersey soon became too small for him, Louis Marchand enrolled him in the sky and garnet colours of CS Bourgoin-Jallieu.

The club was then playing in the 2nd division. Marc played briefly in the youth team, but given his talent, explosiveness and toughness in battle, he joined the senior team in 1977. He was only 17 at the time.

Despite his young age, Cécillon gradually became one of the key players in the Sky and Garnet pack. Indeed, while he was increasingly impressive physically, he was also proving himself to be an exemplary, hard-working and protective player. His teammates were unanimous: despite his young age, 'Marco' was a guy you could count on, whatever the match, whatever the situation. He's a fearless lad who never ran away.

Between the end of the 1970s and the beginning of the 1980s, CSBJ moved up through rugby's top three national echelons Then, from the 1984/85 season onwards, the club, deeply rooted in its home region, settled definitively into the Group A first division, making the whole region proud.

The collective grew in strength over the years, reaching the last 16 twice in 1985 and 1987. Marc Cécillon, as solid in the second row as he was in the third, became, from season to season, the unifying element of this group of proud and irreducible villagers. A fierce fighter, he shone on the screen but remained true to himself. Marc didn't say much, but he stood out for his selflessness and dedication to his team.

In 1988, Bourgoin once again missed out on the finals. The group did not lack enthusiasm but needed a little more maturity. Individually, Marco the Homeric still dominated the proceedings. He is recognised as one of the best and most rugged forward players in France.

So it was that during the 1988 5 Nations Championship, on 20th February, in the match against Ireland, the native of Isère took up the position of wing forward in the French pack. After more than ten years spent scouring the pitches of France, Cécillon had just earned his place in a squad that had played in the final of the first Rugby World Cup the previous year. As Marco made his entry into the Parc des Princes, a television crew was present with his family, who had stayed behind at home. His wife Chantal, dressed to the nines and radiant in her white suit, told the camera how nervous she is to see her husband on television defending the national colours.

Cécillon, 28, was a little late in getting his first cap. Some would say that this interminable wait was due to a yellow card picked up in 1977, in his youth, during a frightful general brawl between Bourgoin and Perpignan.

Although this dark story delayed his integration into the French team, he would become an essential member of it. For the same reasons that he was an undisputed leader of the Sky and Garnets: he was an outstanding fighter, coupled with a personality that was much appreciated by his teammates. He's like a protective father to everyone.

Following his successful debut for the Blues (France won the 1988 5 Nations Championship), Marc embarked on the national team's tour of Argentina in June of that year. France played 8 matches in three weeks. The Rooster and Pumas were evenly matched, each winning a test match. The fearsome team from Tucuman province also caught Les Bleus (18-18), but the latter won all their other matches against other clubs or local teams. Before packing up, the French made a detour to Asunción, Paraguay, where they soundly beat the Yacarés 106-12. All in all, their South American tour was a great success.

Building on this momentum, the Tricolores re-took the 5 Nations Championship the following year. Cécillon was among them, twice wearing the number 6 jersey against Ireland and England.

The same England faced France in the quarter-finals of the 1991 World Cup in a match that would go down in history.

Proudly wearing his 32 years, Marco was taking part in his first World Cup and considered it a pinnacle. However, he did not take part in the group stages. The Cadieu-Roumat pairing performed well, while the experienced Eric Champ oversaw his young back row mates Benazzi and Roumat. But just as it was confirmed that the quarter-final would see the two arch-enemies go head-to-head, Dubroca, the French coach, changes his line-up. He knew that, as usual at the time, this "Crunch" would be a merciless battle. He needed to put up the stiffest possible resistance to the English. Marc Cécillon, with his athletic physique and boundless determination, was preferred to Abdelatif Benazzi.

The Berjallian was fielded as number 8. Everyone was counting on him to weaken the opponents' line of defence. No need to be asked twice; putting up a terrific fight. Marco and the opposing back row were mercilessly going head to head.

The Frenchman launched the hostilities. In the 7th minute, just as the Red Roses initiated a potentially dangerous open-game move, Cécillon broke the deadlock. He destroyed his direct opponent, Teague, with a furious tackle to the chest. But undoubtedly carried away by his desire, he did not bend low enough, and his action was penalised by the referee.

England take control of the score. The match is stormy. The fouls rained down, and the questionable refereeing only made the situation worse. England's back row took their lumps, kept their heads down and eventually fought back.

In the 48th minute, as the Blues were laying siege to the England in-goal, Winterbottom landed a masterful kick to the head of Cécillon, who was helplessly pinned to the ground. Then, from the ensuing scrum, it was

Skinner's turn to vigorously repel an exit from Marc. It was a battle of the Titans that day. A battle in which anything goes.

No matter how hard Marco tried, France lost that day. For many observers, the refereeing had outrageously favoured England. Admittedly, the refereeing was not of the highest quality. But let's also acknowledge that a number of infringements and the French's foul games were not whistled.

However, Mr Bishop's mistakes were just the scrape goat. The France group, plagued by internal troubles, simply missed out on this World Cup.

When Pierre Berbizier took over the reins of the French national team, he made a number of changes. He did not retain the senior players who wished to retire, such as Serge Blanco. He also carried out a purge, but above all, he tightened the group around a fundamental value that had been lacking in recent years: fighting. Commitment, although collective, begins with the individual. Marc Cécillon fully incarnates this spirit and becomes one of the core elements of the France XV.

In 1992, Berbizier appointed the colossus as captain on 5 occasions. The man had not become more loquacious but was more than ever a role model with unfailing commitment, who rallied around his fatherly figure in this group in reconstruction. He seemed to protect the whole team with his solid but discreet wing, acting as a crusader when necessary. That's how flanker Philippe Benetton described his teammate and friend: "He solved certain problems that we were able to solve ourselves at one time... it was clean and tidy. He was highly respected both nationally and internationally. (...) He wasn't a leader of speeches. He wasn't someone who talked a lot. He was someone who set an example on the pitch. As soon as he touched the ball, that's when he expressed himself best."

The Berbizier method quickly produced its effects. Cécillon found himself at the heart of a group in the throes of renewal, from which some exceptional players were emerging. Marco and his band would travel to the 4 corners of the globe to terrorise teams reputed to be unbeatable.

In 1992, Hueber, Lacroix, Penaud, Saint André, Sella, Merle, Cabannes and consorts contested 8 matches during a tour in Argentina. They brought back 5 victories from South America, winning the two official test matches against the Pumas.

The following autumn, Naas Botha's South Africa, back on the international stage, beat France 20-15. Les Bleus bounced back the following week. They rose to the physical challenge and beat the impressive Springboks 29-16.

The good run continued at the start of 1993. The captaincy fell to Jeff Tordo, who was just as exemplary but, it has to be said, more communicative than Cécillon. The latter wasn't offended; it was quite the opposite, in fact. He remained proud of having 'made the shot', of having been there when the going got tough. He appeared in every match of the 1993 5 Nations Championship, which France won and came within a whisker of a Grand Slam.

The French team would be the first to return to play in South Africa since the Apartheid sanctions had been lifted. On the menu were 8 matches, 6 against clubs, provinces and the Springboks B team. The other 2 promised to be much tougher; they were two official tests against a Springbok team that had already begun its transition to professional rugby and was preparing with all speed to become world champions.

The first test, in" Durban, ended in a 20-20 draw. In the second, on 3rd July at Ellis Park, the home side crashed to a halt. They found themselves cornered by hungry Frenchies, who pushed them to the limit. Thierry Lacroix, the unflappable scorer, put the finishing touches to his gang's domination by scoring 15 points.

However, it was only a short step before the match became a tense affair. As the final quarter of the match approached, full-back Theo Van Rensburg tried a drop-goal after a confused move, but it went wide. And just as the ball was bouncing wildly in the French in-goal, Aubin Hueber popped up to flatten it a fraction of a second before James Small.

Then, in the 79th minute, the same – unfortunate – Van Rensburg attempted a 49-metre penalty kick, which passed under the bar for a few centimetres. The rugby gods were on the side of the French, who won the game by a tiny point, 18-17. Marc was there, of course. He played in his favourite style, right at the heart of the battle, giving his body away without thinking.

When Australia, the reigning world champions, took part in a series of two tests against France at the end of 1993, the valiant Marc Cécillon was also on board. Both teams won a game, with the promise of a rematch as soon as possible.

However, that would not be for a while yet, as the Roosters' next summer tour took them to Canada and New Zealand. Completely uninhibited, they set out in style to give the world's most feared team a run for their money. They disposed of the All Blacks first at Lancaster Park in

Christchurch (22-8), then a second time a week later at Eden Park in Auckland.

Marco came on in the 60th minute of the first match but did not play in the second. As a result, he missed out on the chance to take part in the action that would lead to the masterful 'try from the end of the world'. But this anecdotal miss would not mar the flavour of his selection for his second World Cup.

After having mauled all the major rugby nations, the French national team was now a serious outsider for the title of world champions.

Cécillon did not play in all the group matches, but, as usual, he was there when the pack needed power and ruggedness. He started against Tonga, did not line up against the Ivory Coast, and came on as a substitute against Scotland. He "takes his place" for the rest of the tour, which would end with the mythical and controversial semi-final against the Springboks.

After a disappointing end to the World Cup, Marco retired from international rugby. He now has 46 caps for his country. On the eve of his 36th birthday, one might imagine that he was preparing to do the same with his club. Far from it because the man was still green, and he was preparing to live out with CSBJ the club's most glorious moments.

***

In 1992, while the French national team was restructuring around Marc Cécillon, his club Bourgoin-Jallieu qualified for the last sixteen of the French championship. And even though the Isère men's outfit lost 15-7 to US Dax, the future was still bright for them.

The Sky and Garnet squad continued its gradual rise to prominence and expanded around the fatherly Marco. The solid Michel Malafosse signed for Bourgoin, as well as Kiwi Nigel Geany, who would be joined by his former Wellington team-mate David Morgan the following season.

The coaching staff also moved up a gear when Michel Couturas took over the bench in 1993. He organised the system of play and, with the support of president Pierre Garnier, made a major recruitment campaign, albeit a judicious one. Priority was given to young talent from the surrounding region.

After a final stutter in 1994 (elimination in the quarter-final of the championship), CSBJ was getting into orbit from the 1994/95 season.

Marc Cécillon, installed in the "cage" in the second row, was more than ever suited to the role of courageous captain. The group, put at ease by this unshakeable colossus, played the first semi-final in its history against Stade Toulousain and its host of stars.

On 22nd April 1995, Marc Cécillon burst like a bullet from the corridor of the Stade de la Méditerranée in Béziers, proud as a hussar. The clash with Toulouse was shaping up to be a Dantesque affair. It would be dramatic for the Berjallians.

Tom Thumb Bourgoin was heroic, holding off the reigning French champions to take a 10-9 lead into the 80th minute. Unfortunately for CSBJ, after Christophe Deylaud missed a drop-goal attempt, a confusing action led to a contentious try by Emile N'Tamack.

Bourgoin's magnificent adventure came to an end in a highly questionable move. The whole of Bourgoin city was inconsolable. The scar was so deep... And if the bitter Sky and Garnets players finally bite the bullet, they vowed to go and trod the turf of the Stade de France together, and without delay!

They would fail to live up to their promise the following season, being knocked out by Pau in the quarter-final. As the saying goes, Bourgoin retreats only to leap forward.

The Berjallian army continued to be strengthened for the 1996/97 season, with the arrivals of international winger Laurent Leflamand, lock Jean Daudé and number 8 Pierre Raschi. As usual, the CSBJ was not recruiting mercenaries but brave men from the local area who were committed to the local ideals.

The Sky and Garnets would be untouchable and insatiable for success. With the advent of professionalism, club rugby was becoming increasingly international. And the Berjallian warriors would have the opportunity to show the whole of Europe what they're made of.

A year after the birth of the Heineken Cup, European rugby authorities conceived its 'little sister'. Initially called the European Conference, then renamed the European Shield in 1999, it became the European Challenge Cup in 2002. As its successive names indicate, it enables European clubs that have not qualified for the H Cup to play international matches.

For the first edition, 24 clubs were divided into 4 pools of 6. Bourgoin would crush the group made up of Bordeaux-Bègles, Swansea, Ebbw Vale, Gloucester and London Irish. None of these five teams was in a strong enough position to stand in their way.

They continued to triumph in the final stage, and on 26th January 1997, they contested a Franco-French final against Castres at the Stade de la Méditerranée in Béziers. Cock-a-doodle-doo! Even the trio of referees was French!

The 10,000 spectators in the grandstands would have to make do with a kicker's duel. For Castres, Paillat scored a penalty and his teammate Savy two. Bourgoin, on the other hand, had a pair of top-class scorers in Péclier and Favre. Between them, they passed 5 penalties and a drop goal. Final score: 18-9.

It may not have been an unforgettable spectacle, but it was a truly memorable performance for the irrepressible Berjallians. Their close-knit team, built up over time, had just won the club's major trophy. Their friendship and solidarity would forever be written in stone of history.

In the midst of these brave men, Marc Cécillon, the clan leader, looked completely absent-minded. As if groggy, he carried the trophy, which seemed disproportionately small in his ogre-like hands. His smile was frozen, and his eyes were sparkling but absent; he didn't know what to say. Emotion overwhelmed him. An emotion he didn't know how to handle.

He savoured the moment. He remained loyal to the club in this small town with a population of just 22,000, where the winters were cold and foggy. The offers from prestigious clubs came thick and fast. But he chose to stay "at home" and lead a band of friends who played for the colours of the jersey.

The celebrations were endless. Marco, 'the one who does more than the third half' according to the local saying, enjoyed the binge right up until the final moments. After this European success, CSBJ had to get back to the grind. The club was on a roll in the championship and was still in contention for the French Knockout Cup, also known as the Challenge du Manoir.

Benefiting fully from their growing experience of playing in hotly disputed playoff matches, the Bourgoin's men seemed more unstoppable than ever. They were set for another French Cup final on 27th April at the Stade des Costières in Nîmes. The team from Pau, an old acquaintance of Bourgoin, was the second team to qualify for this crucial match. The stadium was almost full. The stands were predominantly coloured in light blue and burgundy. The CSBJ fans lived up to their reputation as the best crowd in France. To support their beloved team, 12,000 of them crammed into no fewer than 140 coaches!

The weather was magnificent. The sun was shining brightly across the south of France. But despite these optimal conditions, Marco seemed worried. During the warm-up, he appeared with a wide scrum cap covering his entire forehead. Although he was concentrated and determined, you could detect a hint of anxiety in his low-slung eyes.

Was it a premonition? In a bitterly contested match, Section Paloise put up stiff resistance and finally crucified the CSBJ in the 75th minute with a try from Dantiacq.

The disappointment was terrible for Bourgoin, who did not lose out but were unable to organise their game together. Cécillon summed up the match quite simply and accurately: "We struggled to cope with the pressure. We played completely the wrong way round."

Despite this setback, the band of die-hards soon pulled themselves together. The major challenge of the season, the playoff of the French championship, was to begin shortly afterwards.

Having several irons on the fire, Bourgoin tops its group in the regular phase. It then overcame AS Béziers in the last 16 and exacted revenge on Pau by winning the quarter-final 24-18.

For the last final played on the Parc des Princes pitch, Marc Cécillon, as usual, would start in the second row, proudly wearing the captain's stripes. Once again, he would be spearheading a team contesting its third final in four months! A feat that no club has achieved in the past. But it's a feat that should be sublimated by bringing the Brennus Shield home.

CSBJ was preparing to take on an old acquaintance, Stade Toulousain, who was also the defending champions. A clash that sounded like revenge. The nights of Marc Cécillon, as well as many of those involved in 1995, were still haunted by N'Tamack's questionable try.

A tense-faced Berjallian captain introduced his team to the President of the Republic, Jacques Chirac. Favre, the scorer, had been injured for some time. Laurent Leflammand, the international winger and try-hunter, was playing with a broken nose, loosely protected by a mask and helmet. The official's handshake in greeting the masked winger made all the headlines.

The Isère warriors were playing to their strengths. Rallying around their charismatic captain, they were relying on an effective ball conquest and a heavy engagement of the forwards.

But the Toulousans offered solid resistance, repelling their opponents' attacks and playing on the counter-attack. Marco takes part in every offensive. Forgetting the number 4 sewn into his back, he was everywhere. Pushing in the mauls, giving close support, playing open, tackling, passing, and defence-breaking. This final was the last of the season, but it could also be the last of his career. He didn't want to have any regrets.

However, this outpouring of energy would not be enough. There would be no apotheosis for Marco and his band. The dream of a historic treble was dashed. Stade Toulousain, on the other hand, achieved the unique feat of winning 4 French championships in a row.

Years later, Pierre Raschi would sum up Toulouse's strategy coolly: 'They simply made it impossible for us to play'. Mazille, the Berjallian scrum-half, believed that his team had already played its final the week before and that the collective mindset had failed to rise to the occasion: "It is often said that a final is won or lost before it is played, and I think that was more or less the case."

Cécillon considered retiring the following season. But that year, his club struggled and failed to reach the championship playoffs. Marco did not want to leave by the back door and felt that the group needed him to bounce back. Incredibly resilient, with the motivation of a first-teamer and more athletic than ever, he returned to the team. The passage of time was no problem at all. The only clock he recognised was the one that stops at 80 minutes and starts again from scratch the following weekend.

By granting himself another season, the warrior from the cold lands of northern Isère wanted to retire with a sense of duty fully accomplished. Although he left the captaincy to Pierre Raschi some time ago, he was still at the helm of the pack, with his number 4 on his back. And, well, it would also be an opportunity for him to finish with a triumph.

In the European Conference final, AS Montferrand beat Bourgoin 35-16 to deny Cécillon a final European trophy.

The ultimate gift for any player in the French championship would be to retire by winning the Brennus Shield. Marc clung to that hope, having lived and breathed rugby since childhood.

Bourgoin got off to a shaky start to the season, qualifying for the knockout stage at the last minute. The latter goes much better, and after overcoming Bègles-Bordeaux in the quarter-final, the CSBJ found themselves once again up against Stade Toulousain in the semi-final.

Not betraying their reputation, they played with their hearts. Refusing to give up, the unfortunate did not realise that they were becoming blunted and exhausted in the face of Toulouse's terrible organisation. A few bursts of pride kept their hopes alive, but Toulouse was too organised and knew how to rack up the points. Marc came out of his last confrontation with his toughest opponents defeated.

In a career that was refusing to come to an end, Marc Cécillon would have one last opportunity to shine. On 5th June 1999, at the age of 39, the eternal Marco wore the colours of his beloved club one last time in the French Knockout Cup final.

Unfortunately, fate seemed to be playing tricks on him by denying him a glorious exit. For his last outing with his band, Cécillon lost to the Stade Français 27-19.

Marc Cécillon may have been considered re-signing for a while, but without really believing it. He now needed to face the facts. He was the cornerstone of a team that enjoyed one of rugby's greatest epics. He had been the leader of a pack of fearless, unapologetic and uninhibited friends who had almost succeeded in toppling mountains. But this magnificent story had to come to an end. He had to make way.

Some people see retirement from sport as an excellent opportunity to take a step back and enjoy a well-earned rest. Marco, on the other hand, felt it was a heartbreaking experience. Although surrounded by loyal friends, he sank alone into a deep boredom, which would lead to tragedy.

10.2

Marc Cécillon: How anonymity can be a road to hell

Between passion and reason, Marc Cécillon has always chosen passion. It was what had taken him to the highest level of rugby. A reasonable person, even one built like an athlete, would never have reached the pinnacle of rugby. A level-headed player would never have rallied around him one of the most talented generations of his club, CS Bourgoin-Jallieu. A pragmatic competitor would never have brought stadiums to their feet; he would never have become a living god in his region.

A party animal through and through, Marc was as devoted to the party as he was to the pitch. He showed himself to be as solid on the grass as he was unstoppable in front of a load of bottles to be emptied. The Berjallian rock lived his life like a big party full of guests. But when the last guests left and the lights went out, he found himself alone, in the dark, with a terrible hangover.

Just after retiring from the grounds, a certain hustle and bustle kept Marc on his toes. At the request of Pierre Martinet, the club president, he became an ambassador for the CSBJ. After all, who better than him to take on this function? A grandstand in the Stade Pierre Rajon, the home of the Sky and Garnets, is also renamed after him.

Until then, Cécillon's life had been imbued with the glory and applause of the crowds, but inevitably it changed. The decades spent at the forefront of the fight, on all the stadiums of France and even of the world, seemed eternal. However, what goes up must inevitably come down. Cécillon's flamboyant career was no exception.

In the twilight of his career, the Frenchman launched a clothing line. But unlike Franck Mesnel and his Eden Park brand, the venture flopped. He then took on the glitzy role of sales representative for a company that installs artificial turf. With his name as a business card, the contracts would seem to be signed in advance.

Unfortunately, it turns into a cold shower. He was able to make very few sales. When the FFR rejected his application to fit out his fields, he went so far as to fall out with some of the body's executives, interpreting their refusals as a personal attack. Marc Cécillon then would make what he knew how to make and which he always made: to play rugby.

He took up his boots again as player-coach of US Beaurepaire, a top amateur club in the Lyon region. However, these new responsibilities could not fill the emptiness in his life. The transition to a life away from the spotlight proved to be a far more difficult challenge than he had expected; far more fearsome than the most violent of shocks, than the most destructive of the tackles he had to withstand.

Melancholy, he attends amateur matches around Bourgoin. In fact, he was an excellent customer in the refreshment stalls of these small country stadiums. People flocked there to say hello to 'Marco', the unbreakable, the man of honour. Then, after scouring the local bars and drinking more than he should, he ended up in the few joints that were open on Sundays. And situations often escalated; things got out of hand. Alcohol, which should be a party companion, was actually a catalyst for all the fury contained in that 115 kg of flesh. And has been for as long as the collective memory can remember.

Drinking was undoubtedly Marc Cécillon's Achilles heel, even when he was at the height of his career. Once imbibed, the roughness he showed on the field was transformed into a dark and unjustified aggressiveness. When the ethanol took its toll on his system, the quiet, gentle person became uninhibited and turned into an uncontrollable beast. With his party mates, the number of slaps they handed out and the number of establishments they wreaked havoc with was immeasurable.

These epic stories did not go beyond the borders of the region. Everyone remained discreet on the matter. When someone heard that Marco and his cronies were behind another brawl, everyone shook heads in bewilderment and smiled. Everyone forgave everything to the enfant terrible of Saint-Savin. And if no one forgave, everyone was content not to see, not to want to know.

His entourage constantly, and quite culpably, calmed things down. Thus, René Berchemin, President of the CSBJ in the 1980s and godfather to one of Marc's daughters, was an influential lawyer. On numerous occasions, Maitre Berchemin was forced to cover up the consequences of his player's excesses. Each time, he had to sign substantial cheques to compensate for the damage and avoid lawsuits.

On another occasion, during a trip to Biarritz, Cécillon returned home drunk in the early hours of the morning on the day of the match. As the press learned the reasons for this, the journalists were summoned to a rather special meeting with the CSBJ management. During this discussion, they were expressly asked, if not ordered, not to divulge anything about the misdeed. Once again, a veil of guilty compassion was cast over his excesses, over his nocturnal outings that turned into Visigoth raids. Once again, everyone turned a blind eye to the binge drinking, the destruction and the brawls just as they turned a blind eye to the extramarital affairs.

Since then, when things got out of control and the situation was irreparable, the only solution was to call on Louis, Marc's father. He's the only one who could talk some sense into him when he's under the influence of alcohol. The only one.

The months and then the years passed after Marco retired from the highest level. As time passed, he became increasingly anonymous. He felt like a stranger in a world he used to dominate until recently. Drink and drugs became his refuges. But they did not stop him from continuing his escapades. More excess, more violence. His behaviour, which had been tolerated during his years of success on the pitch, became an insidious demon, firmly rooted in him after his retirement.

Those closest to him, particularly his wife and daughters, were disillusioned and powerless witnesses to his descent into hell. However, the term 'witness' is a misnomer. The term 'victim' would be more appropriate.

Chantal discreetly turned a blind eye to his behaviour. She asked no questions when Marco disappeared for days at a time. She took the insults in her stride and vehemently protected her daughters from the outbursts of violence when her husband broke everything in the house in a fit of rage. "The less we saw of him, the better off we were", her youngest daughter Céline would say later.

In 2003, the former Berjallian icon was nearing the bottom of the abyss. He was drinking in ever-increasing quantities and overusing antidepressants. He swallowed capsules of Loxapac, a potent neuroleptic, like Halls for a sore throat. According to his nearest and dearest, he was developing symptoms akin to paranoia. He completely lost his bearings in a universe where he no longer fit in.

Chantal's mother tried, gently and appropriately, to persuade him to consult specialists to help him begin the healing process, to no avail. Powerless, she had to settle for offering her daughter asylum when the marital crises became too violent.

Chantal, quite rightly, could take no more. While her husband wandered, she took the courageous decision to free herself from this violent and destructive hold. She laid the foundations for a new life without him, this illustrious husband who was adored by the masses but feared within his own household. She successfully resumed her studies in the medical sector and closed her clothing shop. This boutique, created with the support of the CSBJ to keep Cécillon in Bourgoin, was a symbol that brought back too many bad memories.

She soon landed a job as a medical secretary in Lyon, the big city in the region, some forty kilometres away. This opened up new perspectives for her as she met new people and developed new interests.

Because of her work, Chantal was less involved in the marital home. Perhaps this was a way of avoiding being targeted by a husband she no longer recognised. The situation between them became even more heated when the betrayed wife she once was decided she would no longer turn a blind eye to Marc's countless sexual encounters. She refused him and stayed in separate rooms. Sometimes, she had to lock the door in the illusory hope that this thin plank would withstand an assault from the drunken colossus.

For his part, Marc couldn't stand the fact that his wife was no longer under his thumb. He couldn't accept that she wasn't entirely devoted to his sole service. He couldn't imagine Chantal being happy without him. In fits of paranoia, he imagined she was cheating on him. Sometimes, in a fit of rage, he barged in during one of his wife's gynaecological consultations, thinking he had found an adulterous couple. This was not the case. As investigations would later confirm, his wife was blameless and did not have any extramarital affairs.

When, in June 2004, in yet another outburst of temper, Marc pulled out a revolver and shot into the air in the garden in the presence of his wife and eldest daughter Angélique, the point of no return had been reached. During the following month, Mrs Cécillon consulted a lawyer. She wanted to divorce him and live without him.

While the former rugby player was sinking into a deep – albeit hardly perceptible to his inner circle of friends – depression, his wife was opening up a whole new world of possibilities. She finally allowed herself to broaden her horizons while her husband's narrowed. Their two destinies thus crossed in the emotional lift. Marc Cécillon didn't accept this.

It was the beginning of August —the 7th, to be precise. On the shores of Lake Vénérieu, in the mildness of a late summer afternoon, a game of pétanque between friends was drawing to a close. Marc Cécillon finished his glass of pastis and got on his Harley Davidson. He was expected in Saint-Savin, a stone's throw from where he was. The Bejuy family's close friends were organising a party at their home that evening. The magnificent weather lent itself perfectly to the gathering. The evening promised to be superb.

The former CSBJ captain arrived on site before 8 pm, a bottle of pastis under his arm. Around sixty guests were already there. All of them were rugby players or were involved in rugby circles. The Berjallian colossus was very much at home in this world. His wife, Chantal, had also already arrived.

The hours ticked by, and Marc had one drink after another. The alcohol slowly got him drunk. Unusually for a man who didn't open up much, he confided in some of the guests about his marital problems. Then, as time went by, he became unpleasant and short-tempered. Everyone at the party knows how unpredictable he could be at times like this. Nobody paid any attention to his sharp, aggressive remarks. His words became less and less coherent, to which awkward silences responded. Once again, everyone forgave him everything; everyone looked the other way all the more so in a situation like this, where nobody wanted to expose themselves to his wrath.

As was often the case at such gatherings, the aperitif drags on. At around 11 pm, the hosts asked their guests to join them at the table. Marco, who was drunk, showed himself to be discourteous towards Chantal. Elisabeth Bejuy, the lady of the house, intervened. Their argument escalated. 'You don't scare me,' she threw at him. In response, he slapped her across the face with his gargantuan hand: 'It exploded in my head. I was stunned', she recalled.

Christian Bejuy didn't back down. He threw two punches at Cécillon. Out of his mind, and certainly disappointed in his friend, he shouted: 'Who are you going to hit now?!'

The tension came down a notch. Christian took the opportunity to demand that his friend Marc should leave. Marc, shameless as a child caught with his hand in the cookie jar, obeyed and apologised to his host.

Nevertheless, the spurned guest reappeared half an hour later. Seeing him approaching, Christian Bejuy took the initiative and stopped him. But Cécillon seemed to have come to his senses. 'He was calm. He told me he wanted to say hello to a few people before leaving. I didn't know he was armed'. In fact, at that moment, nobody knew that Marco had returned to his home in Saint-Chef, a village just next door. More importantly, no one suspected that a Taurus 357 Magnum was hidden under his T-shirt. A gift he received on his famous tour of South Africa in 1993, and he brought it back with impunity in his luggage. Once again, his aura had given him a free pass. Once again, someone had to close their eyes to his borderline behaviour.

The intruder indeed greeted some of the guests, but when he approached Chantal, he ordered her to follow him. He wanted to take her to his car to have a conversation. She pushed him away: 'You can whistle for it!' The answer was clearly not what he expected. Frustrated, he drew his gun in one swift movement. Just as suddenly, he opened fire on Chantal, almost at point-blank range.

Five shots clanged. Two bullets hit the unfortunate woman in her fifties, one in the lung and another in the abdomen. The others ricocheted off the floor while the unfortunate woman, who tried in vain to protect herself with her arm, was hurled against the wall by the impact of the gunfire.

Time stood still for a few seconds. The audience was stunned by this sudden and unexpected gesture. Christian Bejuy was the first to react. He tried to tackle his friend to the ground. In denial of the act he had just committed, Cécillon uttered the words 'I love her! Kill me!' After the stupor, several men joined Mr Bejuy. But Cécillon was a healthy man in his forties who had lost little of his athletic build. Boosted by adrenalin and alcohol, he was developing Herculean strength. Delirious, he shouted, 'I didn't kill her! That's love!'

Nearly 15 men in the prime of their lives would be needed to finally contain him. 'We had to throw a cinder block at his back, then hit him with a chair, then slam him face down on the ground,' said one guest. Then, as he kept struggling more and more vigorously, all the while spouting nonsense, the shooter found himself tied up with ropes and electric wires. As this was still not enough to contain this overman, one guest was even obliged to set up a chair over him and sit on it while waiting for the Gendarmes.

They arrived without delay and took away the former local celebrity, who, in a fit of madness, had just committed an irretrievable act. A doctor also arrived on the heels of the police. Powerless, he could do nothing. The wounds were too severe. The bullets had been fired at point-blank range, hitting vital organs. Chantal Cécillon, aged 44, is no more, shot dead by her husband, the man who had sworn to love and protect her. At 12 minutes past midnight, the doctor officially declared her deceased.

Incarcerated in a gendarmerie cell, the shooter and, above all, the victim's husband was fast and deeply asleep. He seemed to have no consciousness of what he had just done. It was the next day, astonished to wake up between four walls, that the gendarmes reminded him of his tragic deed. After analysis, it was established that at the time of the tragedy, the former international had an alcohol level of 2.35 grams/litre of blood.

The French Rugger world remains in 'shock'. Bourgoin-Jallieu and the surrounding area, where Chantal was as well known and loved as Marco was feared, could not believe the news. A lead weight quickly spread over the small town and the surrounding area. It was in these conditions, which seemed unreal to everyone, that the investigation began.

The inquiry was entrusted to the investigating judge in Bourgoin-Jallieu, Raphaël Vincent, and got off to a fast start. The facts were indisputable, but the examining magistrate would be responsible for determining whether or not the acts were premeditated.

At the end of October, Mr Vincent questioned Marc Cécillon. The hearing lasted almost seven hours. Seven hours during which the indicted man, as was his wont, did not talk much. But given the circumstances, he had no choice but to explain himself, to explain this act of madness.

With difficulty, in bits and pieces, he reiterated that he loved his wife and that he didn't want it to come to this. If he drew a gun, it was simply to frighten her so that she would agree to follow him. Then, after bursting into tears, he said in a breath: 'I have to pay'. The former champion's attitude came as no surprise to the psychologist who examined him for the purposes of the investigation. He said that Marc Cécillon had been very quiet, and then that 'with small touches, you can pinpoint the atmosphere. It's the atmosphere that makes things explainable'.

Not far from the varnished wooden floors of public magistrates' offices, a sort of code of silence was taking hold in the surrounding area. The grandstand that bore his name was hastily and discreetly renamed. Attempts were made to erase the Cécillon surname, and the name is conscientiously avoided. Nobody wanted to talk behind the back of the deposed king of the region. At the same time, many people felt a pang of guilt; they resented the fact that Marc never faced up to his responsibilities. When he was scouring – and ravaging – the region's balls, or when he was arrested in a state of advanced drunkenness at the wheel of his car, there was always someone to use his influence and 'arrange the deal' for the local champion.

Judge Vincent then called a number of honourary witnesses to draw up a psychological portrait of the accused in order to determine his psychological state at the time of the events. A succession of Bourgoin rugby men, as well as international players (Berbizier, Tordo, Rodriguez, Lapasset) and members of his entourage, sat in the magistrate's chambers. They all agreed that Cécillon had become more irritable, even more abrupt than before, but there was nothing to suggest that he had sunk into such a state of depression. He never let himself go, always kept fit and paid attention to how he carried himself. Former flanker Philippe Benetton said they spoke on the phone two days before the tragedy. They had even agreed on a date to have lunch together soon.

Finally, in order to complete the enquiries, a reconstruction of the events had to take place. The date was set for 22nd March 2005. The Bejuy villa, where the murder took place, was surrounded by a wall of opaque tarpaulins installed to protect the place from prying eyes. Around twenty witnesses had been called.

Shortly after 8.30 am, Marc Cécillon arrived at the scene in a police van. He was surrounded by 3 gendarmes, ready to restrain him at the slightest suspicious movement. The grey, rainy sky only added to the leaden atmosphere prevailing at the spot.

The civil party, particularly Chantal's family, had high expectations of this reconstruction. They needed answers. Unfortunately, they would be terribly disappointed by the day's proceedings.

First of all, Marc Cécillon, who appeared to remain silent, repeatedly refused to hold the gun and to repeat the acts he committed that evening. It was a policeman who had to play his part. Also, because of his high blood alcohol level on the night of Chantal's murder, he was unable to answer specific questions. 'I've forgotten'; 'I don't know'; he replied several times.

In the late afternoon, a small squad was heading for the Cécillon home in Saint-Chef. Questions were focused on a bullet hole in the ceiling of the house. The prosecution's lawyers claimed that he fired the gun to ensure it was in working order. Richard Zelmati, the former CSBJ captain's lawyer, claimed that the shot was accidental.

At the end of the day, Judge Vincent made his mind up. Concluding his investigation, he sent Marc Cécillon back to trial for premeditated murder. Some of the defendant's statements reinforced his conviction. For example, Marc said that he had chosen this weapon because it was dangerous and easy to hide under his shirt. For this, he faced life imprisonment.

The trial opened on 6th November 2006 at the Isère Criminal Court in Grenoble. The prosecution had to decide whether the fatal act was premeditated. Would the fact that Marc returned to his home and then, it looked like, tested his weapon make him guilty of premeditated murder? Should his blood-alcohol level at the time of the crime be considered a 'mitigating circumstance'? 2.35 grams/litre of blood is a very high level, but the colossus, now an alcoholic, seemed capable of absorbing more. Was he in his right mind when he coldly pulled the trigger?

Everyone began by revisiting Cécillon's story. We talked about his childhood and his immersion in the world of rugby when he was very young. The sport was his only passion and, thanks to the glory it brought him, his reason for living. It was impossible for him to envisage doing anything else but playing.

The accused, with his unusual build, occupied almost 2 seats in his box. Paradoxically, he felt five inches tall, extremely shy, and impressed by the atmosphere. He held his head low and spoke very rarely. If he could, like a turtle, sink his head further into his shoulders until it disappeared, he would. He didn't defend himself vehemently and expressed himself awkwardly. He described himself as a shy person who didn't like to talk about himself. And by his own admission, he had 'difficulty putting complete sentences together'.

Then, it was on to the top brass of French rugby. Bernard Lapasset, the former president of the FFR, as well as Jo Maso, Serge Blanco and Pierre Martinet, then president of CSBJ. During the investigation, they were unanimous. They all described him as 'a generous man and player', 'discreet', 'hard-working', 'formidable', 'extraordinary', 'kind'... Given the circumstances, it was almost embarrassing. Bernard Lapasset felt obliged to temper these glowing words in a clumsy response to journalists: "I've just come to defend him. He has his dark side... I just came to testify".

Listening to these interviews, Céline, Cécillon's youngest daughter, was seething. In her own words, she felt like 'throwing the chairs at the heads' of all those rugby legends who had come to praise the innumerable qualities of the man who had killed her mother.

The Cécillon daughters naturally attended the trial. Angélique, the eldest, was 24 at the time; her younger sister Céline was 22. At no time had they seen their father since the beginning of his incarceration. They would not even look at him. Covered in shame, he didn't dare look in their direction either.

On the second day of the trial, the accused had the floor. This time, he would have to answer for his actions and explain how he came to such an extreme. In his own childlike words, phrases and expressions, he described the extent to which his retirement from professional rugby had left him devoid of meaning. He suddenly felt alone and shut himself away. Above all, he let alcohol become his best companion: 'I should have talked. I've always been a party animal, and at the end of my career, I fell into alcohol (…) I felt humiliated. People would just tap me on the shoulder for a drink.'

After once again proclaiming his deep love for his wife, he admitted that he refused the hand offered by his mother-in-law, Marinette. It was a hand of salvation in the storm but one that he did not want to grasp. She wanted to help him detox. But he never accepted this and let himself be caught up in the demons that had always been inside him.

The court case was not dragging on. At the dawn of the 4th day, the final pleadings were being heard. The verdict was about to be delivered. The facts were in, and Cécillon's defence was working hard to soften his sentence, insisting that alcohol was a mitigating factor. According to the rugby player's lawyers, anyone with 2.35 grams of alcohol per litre of blood would not have full discernment.

Marc defended himself by saying that he sank after his retirement, partly due to the fault of the management of his lifelong club. He said he was deeply disappointed, even hurt. Despite his unwavering loyalty – 23 years wearing the sky and garnet colours – and despite turning down offers of golden opportunities from other clubs, CSBJ left him by the wayside when he retired. Having his name on a grandstand certainly flatters the ego, but it didn't fill an ardent heart, nor did it fill the empty and dreary days of a retired player. Pierre Martinet, irritated to see himself accused of all the wrongs, would have a strong reaction at the end of the court hearing: 'accusing me of not having helped him... damn it, help yourself, and heaven will help you!'

The victim's daughters, who had to painfully face their father, remained united but had two somewhat different approaches. Céline had harsh – but understandable – words for him: 'I'll never forgive you. I don't have a mother anymore'. Angélique, on the other hand, despite her deep grief, asked for understanding. She felt that 'her father has already been punished'.

In her indictment, the public prosecutor requested 15 years' retention. The sentence was handed down shortly afterwards: Marc Cécillon was given a 20-year prison sentence for shooting his wife in cold blood. The judges and jury considered that his act had been prepared.

At the time of the verdict, Chantal's family and friends were left with a taste of incompletion, a bitter sensation. Over the last four days, a trial had been held against a former international rugby player; against the emblematic captain of CS Bourgoin-Jallieu; against rugby, which was becoming professional and had no support structure for young retirees; against the Bourgoin-Jallieu club and its directors; against alcohol; against medication; and against an entire region that closed its eyes to the misdeeds of its beloved child.

Everyone also spoke about Marc Cécillon's distress and recounted his life and professional career. Everyone dwelt on the statements made by these glorious names in rugby who came to praise Marco. Their words were relayed throughout France. Unintentionally, they created a block behind the former captain of the French national team. So much so that the Cécillon girls, who were simply anonymous, felt they had to fight against a corporation of celebrities from the world of rugby. The Rugger elite painted a flattering portrait of one of their own, but only in terms of the player. The one on trial was the man.

Unconsciously, the murderer's personality took up all the space in this court case. There was no tribute to the victim. No one dwelt on the personality of the unfortunate woman; few witnesses had the opportunity to say how this scorned woman maintained an exemplary line of conduct despite the humiliations imposed on her. There was no mention of her strength of character; she who, at the age of 44, drew from within herself the resources to make a fresh start. She wanted to give herself permission to live, but her husband shattered that momentum in a fit of madness. By not mentioning Chantal's personality, her whole person is overshadowed. Overshadowed by the trial of her murderer. That's the last straw.

The media coverage is very much geared towards what will captivate the crowds the most. Very few photos of Chantal are published in the press. There are few articles about her funeral, as she is buried under a tombstone with only her first name engraved on it. The fall of the champion completely eclipsed his most terrible event: the murder of his wife.

Marc Cécillon indicated before the proceedings that he would accept the sentence, whatever it might be. When the verdict was announced, he changed his mind. He announced shortly afterwards that he wished to appeal against the judgement.

The appeal trial opened in Nîmes on 1st December 2008. This time, the deposed rugby star was represented by Eric Dupond-Moretti, a leading figure of the lawyers who were used to high-profile cases and who became Minister of Justice.

In the meantime, Angélique went to visit him in prison. While she considered his act indefensible, she added that this man is, and always will be, her father. As for Céline, the pill was still not going down. The young woman was as virulent as ever towards him. When, with a cry from the heart, she spitted all her hatred in his face, the giant looked down.

In Nîmes, Me Dupond-Moretti proved his status as a leading barrister. He fought tooth and nail and managed to destabilise the magistrates' certainties. However, in this second part of the case, no mention was made of the life and personality of the victim, Chantal, any more than in Grenoble. Her killer took up all the attention, and the victim was once again anonymised.

On 3rd November, the final judgement was issued. The sentence was reduced to 14 years' imprisonment. Eric Dupond-Moretti was convincing, and this time, premeditation was ruled out. Angélique, torn from within, would have a few brief words of empathy for her father: 'This trial was fairer than the one in Grenoble. Justice did its job. I'm happy for my father.'

The defence was equally satisfied with the verdict. The final word would go to lawyer Dupond-Moretti, who summed up the general feeling of this second judgment in one sentence: 'Everyone is locked into this verdict'.

Incarcerated at the Muret detention centre near Toulouse, Marc Cécillon refused to let himself go. Despite the passing years, he had retained his athletic physique more than ever. He joined the prison rugby team and organised matches with some of his former teammates, thanks to his contacts in the rugby world.

Just before the summer of 2011, Marco was going back to the world. After 7 years in prison, thanks to his exemplary conduct, he was granted parole. Solange, his mother, said that her son 'has changed. He's not the same person'. Marinette, Chantal's mother, was up in arms. She said she was disgusted. 'He's getting off lightly, whereas my daughter got life'.

After remaining faithful to the region of his birth throughout his life, the repentant man decided to distance himself from it. He seemed to find redemption in the South of France and in his work as a farm labourer and landscaper. He shared the life of a prison visitor who visited him regularly and wanted to rekindle his relationship with his daughters.

While the scandal faded into the background and seemed to have been forgotten, Marc Cécillon resurfaced in early 2014. Clearly, his attempts to reconnect with his daughters did not go well. The press reported that the father was taking his daughters to court.

The reason? He accused them of 'mismanagement of the family estate'. He was calling Angélique and Céline to account for managing the few properties that Marc owned in equal shares with Chantal.

There did not appear to have been any serious breach of duty or any attempt at dispossession on the part of the two young ladies. Given their young age at the time of the inheritance and the other concerns they had to deal with at the time, they had simply done their best. Their lawyer, Maitre Rodamel, considered the approach indecent. He would succeed in getting the matter settled out of court in the privacy of a notary's office.

In the end, this dispute would remain anecdotal. The minor disturbance quickly died down, and Marc Cecillon resumed his activities as a farm labourer anonymously. The lull would last only a short time.

In January 2015, a bomb exploded in the world of French rugby. It almost sounds like a hoax. However, for the people of Bourgoin-Jallieu, who were close to the protagonists of this new development, it was nothing more than an open secret.

Alexandre Dumoulin, a player who was trained at CSBJ and played for Racing Metro 92, announced through his agent and friend – Jérémy Bouhy – that he was none other than Marc Cécillon's biological son! The move was intended to be frank and wholesome. Alexandre began making a name for himself following his first selection for the French national team in November 2014. He didn't want these revelations to be made public in a way he hadn't chosen.

The Parisian player tactfully took care not to splash at anyone. Before revealing his secret, he notified Marc Cécillon, his mother -Carole Dumoulin- and one of Marc's daughters. After this came out, the young man also made it known that the topic was closed and that he wouldn't be saying anything more about it.

Carole Dumoulin would attest to her son's words with simplicity and honesty: 'I was 19, I had an affair with him, I was simply in love, and I had a child. Alexandre was recognised by someone else, but Marc Cécillon is the progenitor. He was married, I didn't ask him to recognised the child, I respected his choice of life'.

There is irrefutable and alive proof that Marc Cécillon had a string of conquests in the region while, at the same time, being sickly jealous of his wife. As Odette, the wife of former President Berchemin, once said: 'Marc was an idol, and he never turned down advances'.

In 2017, the former CSBJ captain was, in a way, rehabilitated by his peers. He was back in the world he loved so much, the world in which he was one of the gods for a few years. As former Bourgoin-Jallieu players celebrated the 20th anniversary of the famous' year of the 3 finals', Marc Cécillon was all smiles among his former teammates. He would even conduct an interview with the journalists present that day.

But once again, in September 2018, Cécillon name appeared in the press. This time, the facts were far less serious but showed that the colossus was still experiencing particular difficulties.

After a vintage in which he had participated, he saw red, 'shoves' his boss, took possession of a car parked in the courtyard of the property, and crushed another car parked nearby. Apologising, he frankly admitted that alcohol was still a problem for him. And so his life as a retired rugby player continued down a chaotic path that seemed to have no end in sight...

The grandiose career of Marc Cécillon, the archetypal modern forward – fast, athletic and not without a certain flamboyance – has been discreetly shunned on the altar of an act relating to his private life, which occurred when he was already retired from the field. Efforts were made to make his mark transparent, both in the French national team's history and that of the CSBJ. No doubt to avoid having to mention his name; no doubt to try and hide the fact that many 'didn't want to see the obvious'; no doubt to ease the conscience of those who have forgotten that, in rugby, being a teammate is a role played at all times, not just on Saturday nights in nightclubs or at balls. We should give Marc Cécillon his due: he was an exceptional player.

Nor can we remain silent when we realise that the Cecillon affair is, in fact, the 'Marc Cécillon affair'. The unfortunate Chantal had her life taken by a madman who gave in to his baser instincts. She should be restored to her rightful place as a victim, and a sincere and heartfelt tribute paid to her memory.

11

1995: The All Blacks go pale

On 24th June 1995, the final of the third Rugby World Cup was played at Ellis Park in Johannesburg. South Africa, the host country, was facing the fearsome New Zealanders, who counted extraterrestrial Jonah Lomu among their numbers. Before the match, the All Blacks were overwhelming favourites. It was hard to imagine the South Africans standing up to the Kiwi steamroller. But at the end of extra time, thanks to a dropkick from Joel Stransky, the Springboks would lift the Webb Ellis Trophy.

Without in any way detracting from the merits of the South African team, or from the fact that any team, driven by the fervour of its people, can turn mountains upside down, it seemed that the New Zealanders were not entirely up to the task that day.

In the aftermath of this lost game, under pressure from journalists who had caught wind of something that happened within the team, the All Blacks staff finally revealed that a large number of players had been seriously ill over the previous few days. And that was why supersonic winger Jeff Wilson, still suffering from a violent bout of gastroenteritis, had to leave the field before half-time.

Two days before the final, manager Colin Meads and coach Laurie Mains decided to dine out, accompanied by the players who would not be playing in the final. Meanwhile, some of the players who were due to play in the match go out to the cinema.

During the evening, Meads and Mains were not feeling well and cut short their outing. When they reached their hotel, they found prop Richard Loe in the garden, suffering from a violent stomachache. When they entered the hotel lobby, Zinzan Brooke came to them with some less than reassuring news. The players had to leave the cinema before the end of the film, many of them feeling terribly ill. On the way home, some were overcome by uncontrollable vomiting, regurgitating wherever possible, whether in dustbins or through car windows.

After a turbulent night for many members of the group, Colin Meads held a meeting with the team management in his room. He decided to stay there because he was simply unable to move. Everyone debated the possibility of asking for a postponement of the final but finally decided to keep the matter under wraps and not to inform anyone of the situation. They didn't want to reveal any weaknesses, and they didn't want to give their future opponents a strategic or psychological advantage.

Mike Bowen, the team's only doctor, would battle for two days to get as many players back on their feet as possible. According to Rory Steyn, the South African police officer in charge of protecting the squad: "At the doctor's, it looked like a scene from the film *Saving Private Ryan*. Players were lying on the floor, while physiotherapists administered electrolytes and gave them injections".

On D-Day, with the exception of a few players, the group had recovered as best they could. However, the mental and physical preparation had taken a heavy toll. As the All Blacks were taking to the field, Brian Lochore, one of the New Zealand managers, was worried and couldn't help thinking that the game would be a massacre. But his team hung on, and regular time expired with the score tied at 9-9. Then came extra time. The score changed, 12-12 until Stransky crucified New Zealand with his now-famous drop-kick.

The story could have ended there, but some people half-heartedly doubted that the acute gastroenteritis was accidental. After the World Cup, Laurie Mains contacted a South African private investigator, whose identity he will never reveal. Despite his pugnacity, the detective was only able to bring to light one fact: a waitress, employed a few days before the start of the gastroenteritis epidemic, mysteriously disappeared the day after the first symptoms appeared in the Kiwis. To this day, she remains nowhere to be found.

A few years later, after some reflection, Brian Lochore recalls an event that puzzled him. One day before the symptoms appeared, the hotel exceptionally had the group dine in a different part of the restaurant from where they usually ate. Knowing that no other guests in the establishment would be affected by gastroenteritis, the fact is troubling, to say the least.

A few months later, Colin Meads comes out of the woodwork, claiming that English bookmakers were behind the plot. He claims that this information originated in London financial communities. With the All Blacks heavily favoured before the match, sports betting operators would have decided to alter the odds to their advantage.

Finally, Commander Steyn, the former South African officer in charge of protecting the Kiwis, would state on several occasions that, despite the high political stakes involved in the competition, "the South African rugby federation has nothing to do with it. And according to the information I've been able to gather, it's the bookmakers who are behind this affair."

No official investigation has been carried out. Similarly, no public figure claiming to have such or such information has, to date, been willing to reveal these sources. All these elements are merely a bundle of "presumptions" to use a judicial term. At the time of writing, only one fact is proven: two-thirds of the New Zealand players were affected by an epidemic of acute gastroenteritis on the eve of the 1995 World Cup Final.

12

Expreso de medianoche: Willie Anderson

It's never too late. Willie Anderson, the son of a Tyrone farmer, knows all about that. On 10th November 1984, at the age of 29, the second rower posed for the first time in a photo of an official match for Ireland, his country. And if Willie was so proud, it was because he thought this moment would never come. Some players reveal themselves late after they have matured. This was not the case with Anderson, whose skills had been known to everyone for a long time. He was one of the spearheads of an Ulster team that would crush the Interprovinces championship 10 years running! There were insistent rumours that the reason he was only appearing in green at a late stage was because he was forced to remain in purgatory for a long period. In reparation for a gross error of youth...

A native of Sixmilecross, in the heart of Northern Ireland, Anderson recently wore the colours of Dungannon when, at the age of 23, he was also called upon to defend the colours of the province of Ulster. He earned his ticket to a squad that would soon reign supreme in the inter-provincial championship. What was more, he would later be called upon to assume the captaincy of his province. Suffice it to say that the young man was well on his way to the top, especially as he showed great aptitude. Cross my heart and hope to see international honours quickly!

The following year, the Irishman was invited to join the Penguins, the eponymous team of an English charity that promotes rugby. The squad was due to travel to Argentina in August to play a series of matches against local teams. For the Ulsterman, this was an excellent way to fill out the off-season.

After two matches against La Plata and the Province of Córdoba, the British reached the capital, Buenos Aires. They faced C.A Banco Banco Nación, the team of Argentinian metronome Hugo Porta.

After this last game, the Penguins gradually left the post-match reception to enjoy the Argentinian nightlife in small groups. No need to worry; the place was safe! And with good reason: the city, like the country, had been under army control since dictator Jorge Rafael Videla took power in March 1976. So the Penguins were off to the other side of the world! Willie, who was not insensitive to the festive sirens, joined a small group that had formed.

The small band visited a few bars without going overboard, according to them. Then, as they made their way to the next place for a drink, they passed an official building, the Office of Information Security. The Albiceleste, the national flag, flew proudly. The sight of this symbol reminded Willie of his adventures the previous summer. On a trip to Canada with Stranmillis College, he had managed to steal a Canadian flag. Like a trophy, it now hangs on his bedroom wall.

Thinking of the cachet, a second flag would add to his decoration. The Irishman considered grabbing the Albiceleste, waving in the wind in front of him. Without a moment's hesitation, Franck Wilson kept watch while another comrade helped him remove the insignia from his mast. History would incorrectly record this famous accomplice as Davy Irwin. In reality, it was a player whose name Anderson did not wish to divulge. In his book *Crossing The Line*, published in 2001, he refers to this character as 'Mister A'.

Delighted with their catch, the three men returned to their hotel. Already tipsy, they planned to continue drinking there. Probably agitated and half-drunk, they didn't notice the strange look on the receptionist's face. He had noticed perfectly that Willie Anderson was holding his 'souvenir', torn from an official building.

As they had agreed earlier in the evening, Willie Anderson, Davy Irwin, John Palmer, Ginger McLoughlin and 'Mister A' met in one of their rooms. No sooner had they finished a beer than there was a loud knock on the door. Half a dozen enraged policemen armed with machine guns burst into the room. They were looking for something that belonged to the Argentinian state and that had just been stolen.

They had no trouble finding the Albiceleste taken by the Ultach. Although the theft seemed minor, the offence seemed serious in the eyes of the police, who roughed up the group of partygoers. Everyone was asked to produce their passports. McLoughlin pulled out an Irish ID. He won't be bothered. But when the other four players presented their documents, the policemen's eyes darkened even more. The affair would not end there.

In the height of poor taste, the four holders of passports bearing the British royal crown chose the wrong moment. They were 'suspected' of having attacked an Argentinian national symbol at a time when rising tension between England and Argentina would lead to the Falklands War less than two years later. Handcuffed, they were taken to a detention centre. The police officers had no taste for the eccentric humour of drunken foreign rugby players.

Strip-searched and subjected to endless interrogation, the future captain of the Irish national team would not be allowed to sit down for the first 24 hours of detention. When he met an embassy official, Willie realised that he would not wake up from this nightmare. He was indeed being held prisoner by the Argentinian junta. 'You don't realise how serious the situation is,' the diplomat told him laconically.

Palmer was the first to be released after four days in prison. The enquiry established that only three persons had taken part in what was described as a crime. Anderson, who was still being held, was being moved from sweaty cells to unsanitary dungeons cloaked in human excrement.

In the uncertainty of his fate, the young man experienced anguish at its most twisted. With the judicial opacity typical of dictatorships, it was impossible to know what punishment would be meted out to him. His country's diplomatic services only sporadically provided him with snatches of information. 'There's a few generals from the junta who'd happily have you executed," he learned from a diplomatic representative. If that didn't work, there was talk of an alternative sentence of 10 years of hard labour in the south of the country. The newspapers, obviously all pro-government, were calling for an exemplary sentence for what they refer to as 'an attack by the imperialists on a symbol of the country'. The firing squad was mentioned, even suggested, on numerous occasions by the national press.

Anderson was scared to death. His cynical jailers enjoyed torturing him. He experienced a near-death experience when his guards threatened him with the barrels of their revolvers at his temple. They also falsely notified him several times of his execution date. Then, when his fellow prisoners were released, the colossus collapsed. It was a severe blow to his morale. Now, he was alone, a prisoner of a hostile regime on the other side of the world. The joke played by a like by a childish teenager had unthinkable consequences. He was in for a real ordeal.

Pending a ruling, the Argentinian court decided that "given the facts of the case" against Willie, i.e. the debasement of a patriotic symbol, the young man could not leave the country. However, he obtained permission to be transferred to house arrest in a hotel. Despite this temporary loosening of the judicial grip, the penalties remained very heavy. In the face of this unbearable uncertainty, some of the embassy's envoys advised the captive to seriously consider 'alternative' solutions for leaving the country. The most commonly used of these included being locked under the floor of a bus to cross poorly guarded borders or escaping by speedboat to other countries.

Totally confused and without any bearing, the Irishman was on the verge of accepting a solution worthy of an action film in order to regain his freedom. Just as he reached the bottom of the abyss, ready to accept the worst, a glimmer of hope appeared.

Some people were concerned for Willie outside the walls of his jail, while Margareth Thatcher's government was distancing itself from the event. This act of mindlessness had become a diplomatic incident and added more fuel to the fire of the government's handling of the Falklands crisis. Anderson would later slip, quite appropriately, and not without a touch of piquant humour, to Denis Thatcher, the Prime Minister's husband: 'If your wife had asked me in 1980, I could have told her there would be trouble about this place.'

On the other hand, the antipodean prisoner could count on the unfailing dedication of those who would become his saviours. Carlos Guarna, the local liaison with the Banco Nación club, did the impossible to obtain the rugby player's release. He even went beyond the impossible. 'He put his neck on the line for me', says Anderson, who remains eternally grateful for his help. Likewise, his lawyer, who was defending a foreignerfrom the UK, would receive terrible pressure to which he would never yield.

Guarna succeeded in getting the local justice authorities to accept that the act had nothing to do with politics. The case would, therefore, be treated as a matter of ordinary law, which suggested a much more lenient outlook. Anderson's defenders pulled it off, and the accused was given a two-year suspended prison sentence. The political furore around this highly symbolic and ill-timed case had ended. After 3 months under house arrest, he was finally freed. He could rejoin his family, not as an illegal immigrant, but as a free man. He ran to hug his mother, who had collapsed morally and started to sink into alcohol at the beginning of his detention.

This return to normality would also not have been possible without the unfailing support of the Sixmilecross community and the Dungannon RFC world. Altogether, in a magnificent show of human solidarity, they managed to raise the – at the time – considerable sum of £10,000 to finance the costs associated with his release. The turbulent local boy owes his people a debt of gratitude.

The lad from Tyrone, though scarred by events, has no regrets. During his long and difficult stay under house arrest, he tried to keep his mind fresh and clear by going jogging around the building and by maintaining written correspondence with numerous people. Among them was a certain Heather. "It is one of those things, the girl that wrote to me, and I wrote to her. We have been married now for 38 years, so it was a happy ending."

Rumour had it that the Ulster lock, once again free to move about, would be 'watched' very closely by his federation. Then, after a lengthy probation period, he would finally be selected for the first time against Australia in November 1984.

Far more exemplary on the pitch than in terms of diplomacy, Willie Anderson would become captain of the Irish team at the end of the 1980s. In 1989, with open brazenness, he defied the New Zealand Haka. The Irish approached the All Blacks arm in arm, close together during their ritual dance. They almost came into contact with them. Anderson stands in front of Shelford. The 2 strong men challenged each other with their eyes, each able to feel the other's breath.

In reality, the operation was nothing of an improvisation. Jimmy Davidson, the Irish coach, had devised a plan to destabilise the terrifying All Blacks! But that's another story...

13

Are the French frightening?

In every sport, there are established tops, or rankings, of players who have accumulated records, such as the number of points scored, the greatest number of matches played, the most caps won, etc. Rugby also has its tops, which can be defined in several categories. First, there are the official rankings, based on tangible figures (top try scorers, top goalscorers, but also the highest number of defeats and points conceded, etc.). Then comes the *consensus* rankings, such as the best tries or the fairest players. Finally, there are rankings of all kinds, left to the sole discretion of those who compile them.

It is to this last section that the indexes of the most brutal French players belong. Several copies were created by Welsh and English journalists, who no doubt forgot that their nations had birthed players like Gareth Llewellyn and Martin Johnson.

In March 2006, a week before the 'Crunch' was due to be played, *The Sunday Times* published its top 10 scariest Frenchmen. According to the English newspaper, the gold medal goes to prop/lock Gérard Cholley, a former paratrooper and heavyweight boxer, for his entire career, described as bloody. The highlight was the knockout of two Scots in a general brawl during the 1977 Tournament.

Also on the podium was the second row Alain Estève, known as the 'Beast of Béziers'. Legend has it that even the touchline referees refused to raise their flags to signal his fouls; so impressive was he to them. Bob Windsor, the Welsh hooker, had a go at him one day: "I gave him one as hard as I could. He got up and winked at me".

Bronze medal for prop Pascal Ondarts, known for his ferocity. He earned his first international cap in 1986 against the All Blacks in Nantes. The match is still known as the 'Battle of Nantes'. He was wrongly credited with breaking four teeth and tearing the scrotum (i.e. the skin of the testicles) of opposing number 8 Wayne Shelford.

Marc Cécillon, renowned for his rugby skills but infamous for having murdered his wife Chantal, and Vincent Moscato were next in line. The 'Beast from Bègles' was suspended for 28 weeks for a frontal scrum engagement incident against England. He would use this suspension to take part in 9 boxing matches.

In 6th place comes Armand Vaquerin, the rough-and-tumble Béziers prop who met a tragic end in a game of Russian Roulette.

The 7th is Laurent Seigne, former hooker and coach of 1997 European champion CA Brive. In the pure tradition of home-grown rugby, he liked to wound up with his props, Armary and Ondarts, before matches. When he became coach, he motivated his forwards in the same way, fighting with them before they took to the field.

Finally, a player who was not a forward appears in the 8th spot: Claude Dourthe from Dax. *The Sunday Times* "thanked the centre three-quarter for his crash, high and late tackles". Along with his son Richard, they are the only father and son to have both been sent off in international matches.

Second-to-last in the rankings is lock Fabien Pelous, who was suspended for 9 weeks for elbowing Australian Brendan Cannon in 2005.

This top 10 concludes with Béziers second rower Michel Palmié, nicknamed the 'Mummy' or the 'Iron Duke' in Britain. According to Welshman Windsor, "he was the man to avoid at all costs". In 1978, during a match against Racing Club de France, he hit Armand Clerc so hard that the latter lost part of the sight in one eye.

Clearly, in rugby terms, the French and the English are the best enemies in the world. This was undoubtedly what motivated *The Sunday Times* to write the article. But then, a few years later, in February 2014, the Welsh media outlet *WalesOnline* also published its selection of the worst French rugby players. The article is titled "10 of the most fearsome brutes French rugby has ever produced".

A few newcomers appeared in this ranking, largely inspired by the one produced by the British weekly in 2006.

The player designated as being the most brutal entered the hit parade directly in the first place: Sébastien Chabal! And with good reason: he hadn't made much of a name for himself in 2006. He doesn't owe this ranking to any out-of-bounds brutality, but simply, he made destroying opponents his trademark. His greatest feats: the disintegration of Ireland's Heaslip during a Leinster-Racing match, a huge crash tackle on his All

Black opposite number Masoe and the broken jaw he caused Williams during a match against New Zealand.

2nd place was awarded to Yohann Maestri for a red card picked up in 2013, following a heated argument with Samoan prop Sona Taumalolo. A few blows were exchanged, but nothing that justified this silver medal.

In 3rd place appears lock Olivier Merle, nicknamed 'Le Massif Central'. The Welsh considered him to be a violent player. In 1995, he butted prop Ricky Evans, who faints, fell and suffered a double leg fracture and ligament damage to his ankle... as well as a broken nose! The French 'Man and a half' was prosecuted and had to pay damages.

Ranks 4, 5, 6 and 7 are occupied respectively by Cécillon, Cholley, Ondarts and Vaquerin for the same reasons as those cited by *The Sunday Times* in 2006.

Daniel Dubroca, the only personality to come to the fore when he was no longer a player but the coach of the French national team, is in 8th place. After the stormy 1991 World Cup quarter-final between France and England, he launched at New Zealand referee Dave Bishop and grabbed him by the throat. It should be noted that the former hooker also took part in the Battle of Nantes in 1986.

Finally, the second row from Béziers, Estève and Palmié close the gap in 9th and 10th place, respectively.

In February 20015, a year later, the Welsh news website added another layer, bringing out a top 16 list of "murderers, thugs and bullies in French rugby."

The players mentioned a year earlier were mentioned again, but the sequence has changed slightly. By going from 10 to 16, new names are added to the ranking.

Gregory le Corvec, USA Perpignan's legendary flanker, is listed in 5th place that year for his "convictions for punching, gouging and headbutting ". *WalesOnline* also points to his "disciplinary record (that) reflects a penchant for a range of transgressions" and presumes that this is probably why the Perpignan man only wore the jersey of the French national team once.

Eric Champ, also flanker, is ranked 12th, not least because of his enmity with his English counterpart Micky Skinner, with whom he exchanged many courtesies during the 1991 World Cup quarter-final. The Toulon flanker is described by the Welsh as a granite player, tough and hardened, with unkempt hair and a highly sinister look, with little inclination to discipline.

Number 13: Franck Tournaire. Described as a prop who isn't "afraid to throw a punch or two", he finds his place on this top because of the accusations made by certain All Blacks after the 1999 World Cup semi-final. After the match, they complained that the Toulousan had bitten some of them and that he had administered eye gougings at others. The Disciplinary Committee completely cleared him of these accusations.

Philipe Carbonneau is number 14 on the list of "murderers, gougers and brutes." A bit vindictive, the Welsh media certainly wanted to punish the Frenchman for the Taulzac brawl, which took place... 18 years earlier! WalesOnline describes him as a player that "knew every trick in the book." Although not as fierce as the other players in the ranking, he is someone "you couldn't turn your back on"

Robert Paparemborde, the prop from Béarn with a black belt in judo and a reputation for being "impervious to pain", owes his 15th place to his hardness and immovability but without resorting to any form of violence.

Last in the top 16 is Perpignan second rower Jean-François Imbernon. Apart from the fact that he enjoyed wiping his studs on his opponents, with varying degrees of application, the reason for his presence in this position is not really explained.

As the saying goes, when it comes to jokes, short and sweet is best. However, the journalists at *WalesOnline* seemed to need inspiration to fill their pages. So, they reheated the topic for a third time in February 2016. Far from nostalgically sharing memories of a time when it was fun to open the slap box, they descended into spite and venom.

This time, it would be a list of 20 names, titled "Murder, gouging and Russian roulette... the remarkable stories of French rugby's most infamous brutes."

The introduction, in the same vein as the title, goes like this: "One killed his wife, another shot himself in the head. Meet 20 infamous brutes who earned French rugby its reputation for the dark side."

Previous articles are simply repeated, adding two new players to the rankings.

Agen prop Grégoire Lascubé is mentioned largely because, in 1992, he had the time of his life stamping on England's Martin Bayfield. Bayfield later claims that Lascubé "played Fred Astaire on his head."

Lascubé's front-row partner against England in 1992, Philippe Gimbert from Bègles, is the last addition to the article. So, if the various rankings are to be believed, the entire French front-row that faced the Red Roses in that deleterious 1992 match is to be classified as a thick brute. Unlike Moscato and Lascubé, Gimbert was not sent off that day. But he would later be accused of punching and eye-gouging the English.

The vast majority of the facts describing these players as brutes are, of course, true. Nevertheless, they have all become part of Rugger folklore, which involves an element of legend and overestimation. "Every time we talk about a match that was played on a snow-covered pitch, the layer of snow increases by a few centimetres."

14

Naas Botha, a 1000-faceted diamond

"Give me Naas, and I'll conquer the world", said Danie Craven, the eternal president of the South African rugby federation between 1956 and 1993. Recent rugby history has produced a number of fly halves, each more talented than the last, such as O'Gara, Larkham, Carter and Wilkinson. In more distant history, there was a jewel in the crown who, for many years, was South African rugby's all-time record man.

Hendrick Egnatius "Naas" Botha was born in Breyten, South Africa, in 1958. A gifted sportsman, as a youngster, he was a talented tennis and cricket player, as well as an athlete who excelled at obstacle courses. As a teenager, he had only one dream: a career in North American baseball. After failing out of a sports studies section in the United States, he continued his studies at the University of Pretoria and tried his hand at rugby. As some saying goes, the try will be converted.

Having just joined the North Transvaal provincial team, he caught the eye of the coaches. They selected him to play for South Africa at Under-20 level. Then, quite quickly and quite logically, given his talent, he was picked for the *great* Springboks team. His first appearance in the green jersey occurred in 1980, at the age of 22, against a South American team. The destiny of the fly-half with 1,000 records was on the move. And what a destiny!

Naas Botha's tactical understanding and passing ability were second to none. These attributes would quickly make him a key player for the Springboks and his province. His outstanding kicking ability would go down as one of the most prolific scorers in the history of rugby (among other records, he scored 2,511 points in the Currie Cup). Using either his right or left foot, he was ultra-precise with his kicks and had the knack of hitting drop again in a flash, even under pressure from the opposition.

Such was his accomplishment that, although he stopped his international career in 1992, his record for points scored with the Springboks would not be broken until 2004. To add panache to his performance, Botha set a record of 312 points scored in just 28 matches. South Africa, which was boycotted from the international scene between the early 1980s and 1992, played very few matches. In 2004, when Percy Montgomery matched his performance, he celebrated his fiftieth cap in the green jersey, 22 more than his illustrious predecessor.

Botha's superlatives were not limited to his goalscoring talents. The man also won titles. In his eighteen years at the highest level – remarkable longevity – he played 12 Currie Cup finals and won 8 of them (including 2 shared. The rule at the time was that in the event of a tie at the end of regulation time, the two finalists were declared winners). Greedy, he took advantage of the lag in the rugby seasons between the northern and southern hemispheres, allowing him to play all year round. Alongside the Currie Cup, Botha also competed in the Italian Championship with the heavyweights of the day, Rovigo Rugby. Between 1987 and 1992, he was a major contributor to two successes of the Italian Championship, in 1988 and 1990.

However, his commitment to Rovigo Rugby had nothing to do with early retirement and was in no way philanthropic. Naas Botha's views would not be shocking in today's professional era, but they stood out in the landscape of purely amateur rugby. He openly displayed his desire to make a good living from the sport. His contract with Rovigo provided him with a juicy income. What's more, it has now been established that he received substantial under-the-table payments when he was playing in South Africa.

In 1983, he tried his luck in American football, which was already a professional sport, by attempting to impose himself as a striker. But he would not be selected for the Dallas Cowboys squad. However, since he had made the trip to Uncle Sam's country, Naas Botha signed a – as it appeared, a lucrative - contract with Dallas Harlequins rugby club. He won the Men's D1 Championship with them in 1984.

Unfortunately, success and talent attracted the wrong kind of people. The fly-half, with his eternal teenage face and well-combed blond hair, irritated some members of the public. His detractors accused him, with varying degrees of virulence and objectivity, of depriving his backline of ammunition by overusing his kicking game. Other, more virulent, critics accused him of being lazy in defence, of not liking to engage in contact and of "sending his forwards out to be slaughtered and staying hidden behind, so as not to be dishevelled".

Botha bowed out of the international competition in 1992 with a victory over England at Twickenham, at the end of the Springboks' European tour, which had seen them return to international prominence. He is the only player in the squad to have worn the green jersey before and after the boycott of South Africa. Finally, in 1995, after a final season with his lifelong province, now renamed the Blue Bulls, Naas bid farewell to the stadiums.

One question will forever remain unanswered: what would his already breathtaking career have been like if South Africa had not been banned from international competitions for almost ten years?

15

Broken destinies

Rugby is the school of life. At its most beautiful, this sport encapsulates all the sensations that can be experienced in the course of a lifetime. Although disappointments and other sorrows are rarely permanent, rugby's physical commitment leaves an irreversible mark on the flesh of the players. Injuries and physical suffering are part of their life. So are tragedies. All of which, unfortunately, can be found in this sport.

A surprise guest at the 1995 World Cup, Ivory Coast was a bit of a Tom Thumb against some of rugby's greatest nations. The African team only played once in the competition. What should have been a celebration for the Ivorians turned into a tragedy. The accident involving Max Brito, the Ivorian winger, remains the saddest event in the history of the World Cup.

Max Brito was born in the Ivory Coast. In 1972, he moved to the Landes region of France to join his father, Charles, who had previously settled there. It was in this rugby stronghold that, from 1980 onwards, he and his brothers Patrick and Fabrice learned to handle the oval ball with Biscarrosse Olympique Rugby.

Later, having become an electrician, Max proudly takes his place, every Sunday, on the wing of BOR, which plays between the and. And as the Ivory Coast qualified for the 1995 World Cup, the Brito family is celebrating: Patrick had just been selected to play in South Africa.

However, due to a bad pubalgia, he was forced to decline the invitation and withdraw. For a time, Fabrice was tipped to take his brother's place in the national team. But a knee injury deprived him of this honour. However, their immense disappointment was mitigated by the news that another member of the Brito family would make the trip: Max had just been contacted to make up for their withdrawals.

The Ivorians played their first World Cup match on 26th May against Scotland. For them, it was a tricky start to the tournament. They were unable to hold out for long against an in-form Scottish side. The heavy defeat they suffered, 89-0, would rekindle the eternal debate about the participation of passable nations in major world events.

Max Brito entered the fray at the very end of the first half, replacing Célestin N'Gabala with a knee injury. Having only played in one warm-up match in Abidjian, the adopted Biscarrosse player was now making his first appearance in an official international match. His dreadlocks fluttered in his wake, and his number 16 flocked to the back of his country's jersey; he was a proud man. "It was like a fairytale," he said later.

Four days later, on 30th May, the Ivory Coast were back on the grass to face another great nation: France. Stunned from the 2nd minute by a try from Thierry Lacroix, the Ivorian 'Elephants' had difficulty containing the French XV in the first half. The 28-3 scoreline at half-time suggested that the West Africans were in for another disappointment.

But with their pride stung, the tournament's Tom Thumbs would pick up the pieces in the second half. Spurred on by the enthusiastic audience at Rustenburg's Olympia Park, they scored two tries through Camara and Soulama. Both would be celebrated as victories. Although Max Brito did not score a point that day, he started the match on the wing for the Elephants.

The third match, against the more modest Tongans on 3rd June, was a perfect opportunity to put in a performance. Decked out in white for the occasion, the Ivorian players took to the field more determined than ever. This match would be remembered for other, more sinister reasons.

Just after the start of the game, around the 3rd-minute mark, a Tonga scrum broke out on the Ivorian 40-metre line. The Tongan scrum-half sent a kick over the top, well caught by Max Brito before the 22 line. Brito escaped a first tackle but was caught by flanker Inoke Afeaki. In the following seconds, the forwards rushed to the point of contact to form a ruck. Referee Don Reordan quickly blew his whistle, awarding the Elephants a penalty.

While everyone got up from the regrouping, Max Brito remained lying on his back on the ground as if inert. His teammate Jean Sathicq immediately went to his side, followed by a first medic, then quickly a second. On seeing Jean, his captain, Max simply whispered: "It's over, I'm paralysed". Reordan then turned towards the bench, making a cross gesture with his arms to indicate that the injured man had to be evacuated.

Almost three minutes elapsed between the arrival of the stretcher and Brito's evacuation. It was an endless moment during which the faces of the Ivorians, both on the pitch and in the stands, tensed with deep concern. After this moment, the winger left the pitch, his neck blocked by a neck brace, strapped to the stretcher, accompanied by some scant applause.

While the match continued, with Tonga winning 29-11, the situation was far more delicate for Max Brito. His neck was seriously injured. Without further ado, he was flown by helicopter to Pretoria, where he underwent emergency surgery. The accident victim, still conscious, clearly remembered being kissed by the nurses, who were moved to tears, before entering the operating block.

His neck, badly positioned, could not withstand being buried under this mass of bodies. Despite the operation performed on the fourth and fifth vertebrae, the medical team, powerless, could only note the irreversible damage. Max Brito suffered a serious injury that left him paralysed from the neck down.

Immediately after the accident, the winger was realistic but optimistic: "It was as if everything in my body had been disconnected. I recognised straight away that I was paralysed. But I told myself that I was going to be repaired, that it wasn't that serious."

What is the situation 30 years later? The body of Max Brito, who lived on the outskirts of Bordeaux, has never recovered from the injuries sustained on 3rd June 1995. A tetraplegia confined to a wheelchair, Max had recovered very few of his physical faculties. He was helped by a robotic assistant to carry out the trivial tasks of everyday life, such as turning on the television or surfing the internet. For more complex actions, even though they were basically simple, such as washing or cooking, he had to rely on the assistance of carers.

Physically shaken, the unfortunate man was plagued by permanent tingling sensations all over his body. Psychologically, he had slowly climbed back up the steep slope after a decade or so of malaise. "I'd say I spent 13 or 14 years in a fog where I didn't know where I was. The accident was very violent. But afterwards, I experienced a spiritual enlightenment, and I understood that it was necessary to accept my disability".

More at ease with his fate, Max Brito even considered himself lucky: "Lucky, yes, to have been able to count on an association set up in Biscarrosse just after my accident" (the Max Brito Association). The money raised by the organisation enabled him to retain a degree of independence. So he could continue to live at home. Max would just like to see his family a little more often, especially his brothers and sisters and his children. But he didn't hold it against anyone. "You can't be at my bedside all the time. Everyone has their own lives".

During the 2007 World Cup, the Tonga team presented the former Ivorian international with an autographed jersey signed by all the players in the team. He was delighted by the gift. "It was the only one I missed. I couldn't exchange it after the match".

More recently, Tongan Willie Los'e, who played flanker on the day of the accident, recalled the dramatic events: "The only sound I remember was someone exhaling because of the weight of the players above. We got up immediately. At the time, we didn't know how serious the injury was. I've played rugby all my life, and I've seen broken ankles, twisted knees and other fractures. The cries of pain from the players are deafening. Unfortunately for Max, he suffered in silence.

I was the second player to arrive at the contact zone. We grabbed Max in what seemed like a matter of seconds. We tried to rotate his body so that the ball ended up in our half. Other forwards arrived, quickly forming a ruck. This kind of action happens hundreds of times in a rugby match. I keep thinking back to that moment, saying to myself: "Why this time?"."

Why this time? In a completely innocuous loose scrum, without any opponent committing the slightest reprehensible act. It was Max Brito himself who answered this question, simply, humbly, without rancour, in the words of an eternal rugby fan: "I was in the wrong place at the wrong time [...] But you can't stop playing because it's dangerous!"

As Jean Sathicq said after a visit to the hospital shortly after the accident: "What a strong man Max is!"

***

Same era, same tragedy, but this time, through sheer determination, a happier ending.

In the mid-to late-1990s, Bourgoin-Jallieu was regarded as a village of diehard Gauls, beating up the greatest European teams. At the time, the Isère-based club was even a top-quality provider for the French national team. Glas, Milloud, Papé, Leflamand and Chabal all wore the "ciel et grenat" jersey and went on to great careers. While Jean Daudé was on the same path as his teammates, he was struck down in mid-air by a serious injury.

Born in Nîmes in October 1973, Jean Daudé began his rugby career in his home town. Growing into a sturdy lad of 1m98, he played his first matches at the highest national level with Nîmes before joining Bourgoin-Jallieu in 1996.

Fitting perfectly into the pack of a sky and garnet team in full rush, Daudé contested 3 finals in 1997. The Bourgoin warriors won the first European Challenge Cup on 26th January 1997, beating Castres. However, they lost the final of the French knockout challenge to Pau at the end of April and could not beat Toulouse in the French Championship final shortly afterwards.

Two years later, in 1999, the indomitable CSBJ players were back in the news. Semi-finalists in the Championship, finalists in the European Challenge and the Yves-du-Manoir challenge (French national cup competition) would not be fortunate enough to bring home a trophy. But while they did not win a collective award, some of them were shining and were called up or recalled to the National XV team.

On the radar of coach Bernard Laporte, who was looking for a new lock to partner Olivier Brouzet, Jean Daudé donned the cockerel jersey for the first – and only – time on 4th March 2000. Starting in the second row, he played a good game, and France won 28-16 in Scotland. However, after he received a yellow card, he was not included in the following matches.

Back with his club, the player was back at the heart of the Berjallian pack. On 26th March, CS Bourgoin-Jallieu travelled to the South to take on Castres Olympique.

During this match, Jean Daudé grabbed the ball at the end of a ruck. He tucked the ball under his arm and set off to challenge his opposite number, Ireland's Jeremy Davidson. A loose scrum quickly formed, and the ball was extracted.

As the players involved got up from the ruck and resumed their positions, the audience noticed that Daudé was in trouble. Lying on the ground, he didn't move.

In the impact, the Berjallian's head hit Davidson's hard. Transported to a hospital in Castres, he was diagnosed with severe head trauma. As a result of the shock, a cervical vertebra was severely damaged, creating a haematoma in the spinal cord. Given the seriousness of the situation, he was referred to a surgery unit at Toulouse Hospital within the next few hours.

After a period of observation, the verdict was delivered. It was terrible: tetraplegia. But fortunately, it would be temporary. After several extremely tough months, Jean Daudé managed to turn things around through sheer determination and hard work! "Little by little, I was able to regain most of my abilities," he reassured.

For Jean, such a rugby accident was only due to a bad combination of details: "Arriving a little faster, a little stronger, having your head more or less well placed... If I had positioned my head differently... it's all about details".

In an interview given on behalf of Provale, the players' union, the unfortunate Daudé was somewhat bitter about the aftermath. Or perhaps he was just being realistic: "I had my photo in giant size in front of the stadium for three months... and then one or two years later, there was no one left. Thank you, goodbye and fuck off! There are no other words. You can't expect much from a club when you have this kind of problem. I think it's hypocritical. There is no rugby family. For me, family means people who are there all the time, not people who are there because you play rugby, because you play more or less well. I have friends; there are people I like in rugby, but I don't think you should mix everything up".

Beyond the tragedy and trauma, the return to anonymity, with a battered body and a nagging feeling of loneliness, is a difficult time for all seriously injured sportsmen and women. These few lines, these few pages, are a tribute to them. A few words addressed to them, whether famous or anonymous. A few words to tell them that we are thinking of them.

16

Ireland's two national anthems

Before each match, in addition to their national anthems, the Pacific nations perform a Haka, a ritual dance designed to curry favour with the gods. The Irish XV also follow a unique ritual: at their matches in Dublin, the Greens are represented by two national anthems.

This particularity also has its roots, in a way, in religion and in the fratricidal conflict that divided Ireland.

In 1922, the island was partitioned into two parts. The predominantly Catholic Republic of Ireland (also known as Éire) became independent from the United Kingdom, while the predominantly Protestant Northern Ireland remains under British rule.

In sporting terms, the Irish Football Association then decided to follow the political partition and created two separate bodies. In contrast, the IRFU, Irish Rugby Football Union, refused to accept any split and continues to this day to unite all the island's players under the same jersey.

In 1926, *Amhrán na bhFiann (The Soldier's Song)*, an Irish patriotic song, was adopted as the national anthem of the Republic of Ireland. As the

IRFU is made up of a majority of Irish provinces (Munster, Leinster and Connacht, as opposed to a single Northern Ireland province, Ulster), it was decided that the same song would be played before the Green XV's matches.

From the 1970s onwards, strong political tensions resurfaced, bringing the country to the brink of civil war. Despite this, the IRFU once again refused to split in two and made it a matter of honour not to cancel any matches involving the Irish national team. The players, united under the same colours, kept on crossing the border and playing equally in each of the two territories.

However, in the 1980s, the people's discontent began to be felt on the pitch. The selected Northern Irish players refused to sing the national anthem because they did not feel represented by *The Soldier's Song*. From the federation's point of view, it was inconceivable to be represented by *God Save the Queen* and even less so at matches in Dublin, which would create a real outcry.

For the first World Cup in 1987, the IRFU introduced a new anthem, *The Rose of Tralee*, which was supposed to suit both sides. This attempt failed and brought no one together. This folk song, with its sweet, honeyed harmony, was deemed ridiculous and inappropriate as a preamble to a rugby match.

A new attempt was made for the 1995 World Cup. The federation asked Phil Coulter, an Irish artist, to create a new anthem. Out of his imagination will come *Ireland's Call*, a song which, according to its author, "was intended to unite all the players". Coulter would admit afterwards that it was one of the trickiest things to create, with every word having to be carefully weighed and thought through.

Ireland's Call was warmly received and has been the IRFU's anthem ever since. This is the only song that is played as a prologue to the Ireland XV's away matches. And when matches are played in Dublin, two songs are played: *The Soldier Song* because it is the anthem of the country hosting the match, and *Ireland's Call*, the unifying anthem of a rugby association that has never yielded to political injunctions.

17

Inevitable Professionalisation

Author's note: This article was intended to deal solely with the Lord project, a professional rugby system devised by an Australian journalist in the 1980s. In researching the subject, it became apparent that the ins and outs of this proposal were far more complex than imagined. In fact, this ambitious system of global rugby served as the basis for the organisation of current competitions.

Pulling out the ball of information available to me on the topic, the Ariadne's thread led me to the infancy of rugby institutions at the end of the 19th century. In order to understand what drove a bold adventure on the scale of the Lord project, I felt it was essential to retrace the history of these rugby unions. In their blind quest for sovereignty, they gave birth to XIII rugby, a popular and professional sport from its earliest days. In return, this 'new code rugby' threw down the gauntlet of its twin brother to a sea serpent that was anything but imaginary: professionalisation.

The 5 articles that make up this section dedicated to the professionalisation of Rugger deal with subjects that, although closely linked, are independent of each other. So, despite a few brief repetitions to clarify the contexts, each article can be read independently.

17.1

Birth of the parent institution: IRFB

On 26th August 1995, the International Rugby Football Board announced that rugby would henceforth be an 'open' sport. The adjective was not chosen casually. It replaced a word that still scratches the lips of some of the institution's directors and the ears of some rugby fans: professional.

In so doing, the patriarchal organisation that administered World XV rugby had just unwillingly overturned one of its fundamental principles. The body was cornered and almost threatened with extinction in the medium term. It had no choice but to ensure its survival by reviewing its position on a rule laid down more than a century ago, stipulating that rugby must forever remain a purely amateur sport.

Evolution was ineluctable. Over the last few decades, the IRFB edifice, sometimes castrating, sometimes hypocritical, had continued to crack in the face of the assaults waged by the powerful force of money and those who possess it. Weakened at the dawn of the new millennium, the institution nevertheless remained all-powerful for a long time, harshly imposing its decisions on its members for more than a hundred years.

In the British Isles, in the first half of the 19th century, football and rugby were one and the same. This ball sport, a direct descendant of the game of soule, was fairly widespread, but the rules were far from uniform. Each locality, each guild and each team had its own regulations.

Rugby football and football split in the 1850s. The boundary between the two games became less and less porous. Players specialised, and each sport followed its own path.

A decade later, football took a step toward professionalism and played by its best players. At the same time, the first rugby clubs were created throughout Great Britain. The sport spread beyond the confines of the universities, where until then, it had been practised exclusively. These amateur congregations were formed for the simple purpose of competing against each other. There was no talk of attracting a public. The few spectators who attended matches were themselves former practitioners, and the press only sporadically covered this sport, which was played exclusively by the more affluent classes of the population.

In the space of just a few years, rugby clubs, often headed by industrialists or company directors, were developing an effective structure. These organisations no longer represented this or that group of individuals but neighbourhoods, towns... and nations.

In 1871, rugby became a relay of confrontation between two ancestral rivals. The English and Scots clashed in the first international match ever played on 27th March 1871. At Edinburgh's Raeburn Place, in the presence of 4,000 spectators, Scotland's Angus Buchanan scored the first international try in history, converted by William Cross. The English also scored a try by Reg Birkett, which was not converted. The men from the Highlands thus won... 1-0! Indeed, for a while, only points scored by kicks were counted. This is where the word 'try' gets its essence. Flattening the ball in the opposition's in-goal used to open the right to an attempt – a try – to take a kick at goal.

This event at Raeburn Place was also an occasion to celebrate a birth: the one of the Rugby Football Union (RFU). It would be responsible for overseeing the practice and unifying the rules of rugby, which was also becoming increasingly popular. In Lancashire and Yorkshire, the strongholds of this new sport, as well as the exploits of the rugby men, started to be covered by reports and press articles. Bread and circuses! The working classes were fascinated by these modern circus games.

The other British nations were experiencing the same growing love affair with the oval ball. Imitating their English neighbours, the Scots also set up a federation in 1873 (the SFU), followed by the Irish with a single federation in 1879 (IRFU), and then the Welsh in 1881 (WFU).

Between 1882 and 1883, a British championship was introduced, with teams from the 4 communities competing each year. However, although each country possesses its own national organisation, the RFU remains the governing body. It continued to regulate the rules of rugby everywhere. And even beyond its borders. The Welsh, Irish and Scottish accepted this situation in spite of themselves while they waited for the opportunity to overturn this hierarchy.

The opportunity occurred shortly afterwards, in March 1884. During a match between England and Scotland at Blackheath, the Irish referee awards England a try that their opponents considered to be invalid. The away team threatened to leave the field. Fair play to them; they finally agreed to finish the game and came back to the dispute at a later date.

The disagreement was slow to be resolved, and other stumbling blocks were added to the quarrel. The situation escalated, and the 1885 England-Scotland match was simply cancelled! Witnessing the dispute, the IRFU (the Irish Federation) took on the role of justice of the peace and invited the representatives of the other 3 nations to a meeting in Dublin. The discussion went further than a simple clarification. The aim was to create a supreme international institution which would take over from the RFU in administering rugby regulations.

The response from the British envoys were categorical. They rejected the proposal outright, putting forward some rather vague arguments. England is the mother nation of rugby. Its federation had been setting and administering the rules of the sport since 1871, and there was no question of it being any different! What was more, the country had far more clubs than its neighbours. And by the way, it was quite inconceivable for these English aristocrats to ratify a charter drawn up exclusively, without their help, by their turbulent Irish neighbours.

Never mind! The IRFU, WFU and SFU dispensed with the consent of the 'masters of the game' and created the International Rugby Football Board (later to become the IRB, then World Rugby) in 1886. Insolent as they were, the 3 federations even went so far as to ban their English counterpart in 1887. Over the next few years, they contested the annual 3-a-side tournament. The decision-makers at the IRFB remained adamant that they would not play England again until the latter aligned itself with the Dublin-based organisation.

Deprived of international matches, the RFU feared that rugby would disappear due to a lack of stakes. In 1890, the RFU decided to join the IRFB, although it was careful to secure a significant advantage: it would be represented by 6 emissaries, while the SFU, WFU and IRFU each had only 2. If it could not make decisions on its own, it retained the right to veto decisions.

Rugby's supreme international institution was thus created at the end of the 19th century. Throughout the ages and right up to the present day, it would govern all the rules inherent in Rugger. Sometimes authoritarian, willingly prejudiced and inflexible in certain situations, it was about to embark on a hundred-year war. A fight against an enemy to whom it did not hesitate to make eyes at night: money.

17.2

The XIII as a counterweight to the XV: in the northern hemisphere

In Great Britain, at the end of the 19th century, rugby was breaking away from the world of public schools, the 'executive factories' of the British Empire. The sport, imbued with the chivalric spirit of yesteryear, spread throughout the population. The oval fervour grew among the working classes.

The aristocracy set itself up - and imposed itself - as the guarantor of the rules and the spirit of the game. Facing the massive influx of the proletariat onto the pitches, the elite, fearful of seeing its monopoly challenged, took the initiative. In the same way that the ruling caste governed the working lives of its employees, it organised itself into rugby federations and leagues, which it naturally took in hand. It oversaw the whole of its world, even when its flock was having fun.

These newly-created bodies, which were thought in the upper echelons, would secure access to decision-making positions. In reality, they carried within them the seeds of a populist revolt. By putting certain 'dissidents' in touch with each other, they facilitated the creation of interest groups that would shake up the institutions from the inside.

The separation between football and rugby in the 1850s was achieved without too many clashes. The schism between 'traditional' rugby and 'rebellious' rugby would become a matter of conflict. Everything about this split is a story of power struggles, alliances, agreements and reversals. A real soap opera! This war of secession will lead to the creation of XIII rugby, which will remain in people's minds as a popular sport. Its 'opposite', bourgeois XV rugby, remained under the thumb of its traditionalist leaders, will cling to its precepts, even at the risk of disappearing.

Divorce originated in 1877. It was fuelled by many insidious actions and, as is often the case, was caused by financial reasons. In December of that year, Arthur Hudson, heir to a dynasty of Leeds industrialists, organised the first Yorkshire Challenge Cup (YCC). He invited 16 teams to take part in the tournament. The event was held under the watchful eye of the guardians of the temple, the RFU, who ensured compliance with a fundamental principle of its ethics: no payment of any kind must be made to participants. The healthy spirit that inhabits the healthy body of rugby men could not suffer any degradation caused by a material reward.

Thus, Hudson donated the profits generated to various charities. The Halifax club, the winner of this first YCC, received a trophy, the famous 'T'owd Tin Pot'. The cup symbolised the noble achievement of 15 athletes who put their individualities aside to accomplish a common project. However, the Leeds industrialist refused to award a medal to each of them for fear that the charm might be seen as an individual retribution.

The competition was repeated the following year and attracted an unexpectedly large crowd. Around 11,000 spectators were flocking to the pitch. Most of them came from working-class backgrounds and were keen on these organised clashes, which tickled their inner chauvinist. Many were thrilled to see the representatives of their town or village trying to assert their superiority over their neighbours.

The Yorkshire Challenge Cup was partly one of the reasons why Rugger took off, particularly in the north of England. Because after having been spectators, the labourers were eager to become players. By the hundreds, by the thousands, they embraced this new sport. However, lacking the financial means or organisational capacity, they swelled the ranks of existing clubs, which were run by the local bourgeoisie. The latter, fearing that they would be 'overwhelmed by the masses', took an authoritarian stance, imposing their own conception of the game and their own rules. At the time, these were essentially based on the unalterable principle of amateurism.

To reinforce this hitherto unspoken catechism, in 1879, the Yorkshire County Football Club issued the first rule formally prohibiting any form of payment to players. The Organisation even turned the screws, going so far as to prohibit player transfers if they were carried out in exchange for a job provided by the new club.

These new regulations did not do the managers of the Northern England clubs any favours. They were swamped with recruitments of men from the working class, from which many talents emerged and who were the pride of their teams. Providing jobs was the best way of ensuring their loyalty and attracting other prodigies. Many clubs introduced a payment system to compensate for time off work and time spent playing rugby, as well as injury-related time off from work. For these clubs, in order not to be destabilised, it was urgent to do nothing. So they continued, more discreetly than before, to hand out envelopes under the table.

Unlike the working class, the Victorian bourgeoisie was not short of a few shillings to make ends meet. They did not give up. They saw the fight against any form of payment as a priority. Thanks to the permeability between the kingdom's aristocracy and rugby's top brass, they won their case. In October 1886, the parent organisation, the RFU, backed up the Yorkshire County Football Club's 1879 rules. And it extended them to all local jurisdictions. The Organisation had just laid the foundations for a policy that would remain in effect until 1995. Officially.

The first sanctions were immediately meted out to those who failed to comply, with clubs being dissolved and players banned for 'acts of professionalism'. Even if certain practices persisted, the fear of the police was a strong cure for 'evil'. Rewards, which became harder to conceal, were reduced. The consequences were immediate. The workers, talented rugby players, though they might have been, could not afford to sacrifice days' wages to practise their passion.

Some clubs were floundering with the loss of their best players, or even all of their players (!). Poor sporting results were leading to loss of revenue, leaving many associations in dire financial straits. Exsanguinated, the northern clubs banded together and urged the RFU to amend the October 1886 regulations. For them, there was no question of liberalising rugby across the Board; they simply wanted to offer their members reasonable compensation for 'lost time'.

From its ivory tower, the Rugby Football Union examined the request with circumspection. Let the workers participate if they wanted, but they had to respect the dogma in place. That was it!

Aware that the situation could create upheavals that would be damaging, the governing body's leaders, instead of relaxing the current doctrine, were tightening the bolts even further. 'Their' sport had to remain under their yoke without any possible dispute.

Throughout history, many sovereigns have succeeded in legitimising their domination thanks to facts that are more or less legendary and partially well-founded. The RFU was going to use the same methods! The institution would look to rugby mythology for its divine right of ancestry. There was nothing like using the name of the presumed inventor of rugby and magnifying his story to accomplish this, even if it meant taking certain liberties with the veracity of the facts.

The top members of the English establishment claimed that William Webb Ellis came from the aristocratic class. He came from their world. And he did the sport's founding act - picking up the ball with his hand - at a match between two Public Schools, of which he was a pupil. It was something they all had in common. With such simple reasoning, they took on the charge of ensuring that rugby was preserved in its original, purest form. They, and no one else.

In 1893, a further thrust was dealt to those who were continuing to advocate 'defrayed' rugby. The Cumberland County Union asked the RFU to enquire about a case. A player had changed clubs in exchange for a better-paid job. The parent organisation investigated. Under threat, the majority of clubs in Yorkshire and Lancashire were joining forces. They threatened to secede if the investigations resulted in sanctions. Troubled by this strong protest, the RFU hastily convened a council meeting. The question of remuneration needed to be discussed again. Quickly.

Following a vote, the possibility of compensation was rejected by a large majority, almost unanimously. In this missed rendezvous with history, only a few clubs 'dared' to vote in favour. Although the north of England had a majority of clubs, their chairmen feared reprisals from the authorities. They preferred not to be too outspoken about their opinions. In fact, they were spared. On the contrary, the handful of unfortunate people who chose to vote against the system in place were punished with heavy fines to pay.

Fighting for their financial survival, the Lancashire and Yorkshire unions founded the Northern Union (NU) in January 1895. This Federation, which was more unofficial than official, was responsible for organising a match between the champions of the two counties. There was an urgent need to replenish the coffers left empty after the 1893 fines had been paid. Taking advantage of the libertarian wind blowing in, and before the central government could get its hands on the NU, 22 clubs in the north of England plucked up courage and finally managed to emancipate themselves from the RFU's grip.

In the same way that the 13 colonies of the United States declared themselves independent on 04th July 1776, 22 rugby associations in Northern England formalised the creation of the Northern Rugby Football Union. On 29th August 1895, in the intimacy of a lounge at the George Hotel in Huddersfield, the birth of rugby league was solemnly made official. The divorce from the existing organisations was now complete.

In 1895, the priority was to enable players from Rugby Union member clubs to be paid. However, the 'mutineers' still believed in a future partnership with the RFU. To avoid offending the RFU, they agreed to pay rugby men a maximum of 6 shillings a day.

On learning of the manoeuvre, the RFU's socks were knocked off. But officials could do nothing except protest. What effrontery from those northerners! It would also be powerless to stop the bleeding of players and clubs leaving its fold between 1896 and 1897 to take refuge under the aegis of Rugby Union. The 'traditionalists' remained steadfast in their positions and kept being inflexible. The RFU, whose existence was for a time called into question, would take its convictions to its grave if necessary.

However, the stubbornness of the defenders of purely amateur rugby was not in vain. They managed to save their institution. The RFU stabilised its membership. Better than that, in a smaller circle of influence, its authority was only strengthened. The banished, the dissenters and those who simply wished to cash in on their sporting skills had left for other climes. The connection between its members was all the stronger because they all shared the same visions.

Rugby Union and the Rugby Football Union would never merge. Asserting its difference, the 'new code rugby' turned to XIII in 1906.

The flanker positions and throw-in from touch were suppressed to make the game more open and fluid. Then, in 1922, the Northern Rugby Football Union adopted the more universal name of the Rugby Football League. The two twin sports, born out of the same embryo, now coexist in the sporting scene. Although there were attempts on both sides to hinder the development of the other, XV and XIII coexist. They are like unsympathetic neighbours who, after many years of struggles, finally accept each other's presence.

On the other side of the Channel, preserving the dogma of amateurism was more of a theatrical farce. More free than its neighbours in interpreting the rules, the French rugby federation would only sporadically attempt, and under duress, to curb the phenomenon of 'brown amateurism'. And since each region had its own specific characteristics, the French Federation would have a difficult time trying to maintain calmness in its stadiums.

Like a commodity, rugby football was imported into France via its harbours in the second half of the 19th century. France's port cities were home to many English merchants. They formed communities and played rugby on their days of rest. Initially amused by these new types of entertainment, the locals gradually started to take part. The first club was founded in Le Havre in 1872, but despite this, rugby-football matches between different towns remained rare.

It was not until the 1880s that rugby gradually reached the capital. The few teams that were created were generally under the control of omnisports clubs such as Racing Club or Stade Français. It was they who organised local tournaments, which gave rise to the early stages of a national championship. In 1889, they all came under the aegis of the Union des Sociétés Françaises de Sports Athlétiques, which was also a multi-sport federation. While this Federation was slowly opening up to the French provinces, rugby was gradually developing, still mainly in towns on the western seaboard, such as Nantes, La Rochelle and Bordeaux.

It was precisely through the city of Bordeaux, with its popular Stade Bordelais club, that rugby penetrated the southwestern countryside in the 1910s. The region would eventually become one of the cradles of French rugby and still boasts a profusion of clubs.

At first, only those who could afford shorts and boots and who had the luxury of time on their hands played the game. With the democratisation of access to higher education, during which rugby football was practised, oval fever gradually spread to all classes of the population. The spread of the Rugger would also be helped by the creation of a military championship in 1904, whose players were supplied by conscription for all, and then by the introduction of a mandatory weekly rest day for everyone in 1906.

1906 also marked the first official international match played by the French national team. They met a team from the antipodes, the 'Originals', soon to be renamed the 'All Blacks'. The unfortunate Bleus were thrashed 38-8, but the result mattered little. The match itself was already a major event.

The delicate learning curve for the French was continuing in the following years. They were not able to hold their own against the British Home Unions, but their pugnacity enabled them to enter the Championship. In 1910, the annual British tournament was renamed the 5 Nations Championship. In accepting this newcomer, the RFU even agreed to give up 2 votes on the IRFB Council as a token of its support. It now had only 4 representatives on the Board. However, France would not be invited to the banquet of decision-makers until 1978.

The Great War put the development of rugby on hold until May 1919. At that point, it was decided to turn the page and let life take its course again. A central organising committee was set up to emancipate from the USFSA. On 11th October 1920, this committee was renamed the Fédération Française de Rugby (FFR). Also, in 1920, the French Championship was back on track. The competition had lost none of the enthusiasm it had aroused before the war. For a decade, styles of play and identities were becoming more pronounced, depending on the region and 'local cultural exceptions'. In France, for example, city rugby, with its polished, sophisticated style, contrasted with country rugby, which was more restrictive and willingly brutal.

In France, more than anywhere else, violence is a veritable gangrene that festers in the Rugger. The French are very prone to quarrelling, and they also have an overdeveloped parochialism. Every match is a pretext for brutality. You want to 'pay off' a bourgeois, show your neighbours that your village has more virtues, correct those arrogant city-dwellers, and prove the superiority of your region over another. Anything goes right down to the fatal wrong-doing. In France, people die on rugby fields.

Not a few voices were raised against this savagery, which was almost institutionalised in certain areas. Twelve clubs, including Stade Toulousain, Section Paloise and Biarritz Olympique, wrote a joint letter to the FFR in April 1930. They urged the Federation to take all necessary measures to restore calmness to the French Championship, which was becoming increasingly fiercely contested. The letter, which also contained other complaints, condemned the 'brown amateurism' practised by many clubs.

The FFR was hesitating. Obeying a handful of clubs would weaken its credibility and tarnish its image of impartiality. But these 12 dissenting voices included seven former French champions. What would be the appeal of the Championship if it were stripped of its leading clubs?

The Federation's first action was to preserve the status quo. The issue remained unresolved. However, the protesters' patience was limited.

Faced with this silence, they organised a closed competition, the 'Tournament of the Twelve'.

The FFR kept radio silence. Fed up, the 'Twelve' sent their letters of resignation to the Organisation and united to form the Union Française de Rugby Amateur (UFRA). In response, the FFR reluctantly pronounced the exclusion of these secessionists, who were already doing it alone anyway. Players from these clubs were equally excluded from the French team managed by the FFR.

By letting its best performers go, the national body was losing out significantly. And the problems had only just begun. The demands being made by the small but influential UFRA were resonating, unexpectedly, far from its area of influence: on the other side of the Channel.

For several years now, the powerful RFU, which continued to keep a 'register of rugby customs', had been taking an interest in the French case without managing to interfere in the discussions. The English did not at all appreciate the image that the French projected of 'their' rugby. The matches between the Tricolores and the Home Unions, which regularly turned into pugilistic brawls, tarnished the reputation of this gentlemen's sport. What's more, from their home turf, English decision-makers were unable to prove that professionalism existed and that it was covered up by the FFR. The creation of the UFRA was a real gateway to France for the English institution, which would finally be able to 'see without being seen'.

The 'Twelve', became the 'Fourteen', pledged their allegiance to the RFU, with whom they shared strong convictions. Information obtained by the UFRA and relayed by the British reached the IRFB. The supreme

Organisation finally got the opportunity to bluntly reframe its volcanic neighbours on the other side of the Channel.

On 2nd March 1931, a letter from Dublin was received at the FFR headquarters. Having gathered sufficient evidence, the IRFB notified the French body that the nations it represented would no longer play the French national team until further notice. The argument was clear and logical: the French Championship was out of control, both on and off the pitch. The exaggerated stakes of this competition led to an arms race between clubs, with no serious control by the Federation. What's more, in most cases, transfers were encouraged by barely concealed payments. According to the IRFB, this unbridled quest for victory was even reflected in the minds of the players, who would do anything, absolutely anything, to win. In short, the existence of an over-committed championship was a breeding ground for brown amateurism, which in turn bred extreme violence during matches.

The situation was becoming critical for the FFR. The most prominent clubs were no longer obeying it. Worse still, these sources of international players were no longer feeding the national team, which had to make without its best players. With its banishment from the 5 Nations Championship, it would have to content itself with facing second-rate nations such as Germany and Italy. With XV rugby losing its appeal, many clubs went out of business. Something needed to be done. It was urgent.

With its tail between its legs, the FFR was returning to the UFRA, which was not asking for so much. Although full of good intentions, this second union had not managed to find a miracle formula. The matches in this 'elite' Championship were also the scene of outbursts. With each side unable to foresee a prosperous future on its own, common ground was found. The UFRA ceased to exist in 1932. The FFR now had to focus on restoring its reputation in the eyes of the British, who held the reins.

A purge was organised. The communication stunt was perfectly orchestrated. Unable to afford to 'shoot the lot', the French officials concentrated on just a few players. These 'symbolic' cases became veritable scapegoats who would receive the wrath of God. Among them was first-class international Jean Gallia. But in making an example out of him, they committed a serious error that would bring the 'fox into the henhouse': the importation and rapid spread of the XIII competitor in France.

After starting out with Toulouse Olympique Employés Club, Gallia was recruited by the ambitious US Quillan in 1926 before moving again to CA Villeneuve in 1930. In the crosshairs of the FFR, with whom he maintained very bad relations, the international became the victim of a cabal ["an intrigue" is a more familiar word]. While the FFR had always 'looked the other way' when it came to amateurism, it suddenly regained its vision when the Gallia case was examined.

The native of Toulouse was banned from his sport in January 1933. In addition to receiving direct remuneration, he was accused of having played an important role in the transfer of a player between USA Perpignan and his club, Villeneuve. Jean Gallia saw himself forbidden to play rugby without having the possibility, as in England, of turning to XIII rugby. This sport was not yet present in France. But with a vengeance, the 'banished' Gallia would play a key role in introducing the 'new rugby' to his country.

Kept away from the fields, Jean Gallia was contacted by some businessmen in the autumn of 1933. They had learned of the existence of an 'alternative' form of rugby, one that escaped the strict - and arbitrary - traditional regulations. In addition to giving its players greater freedom, this form of rugby league was a hit abroad and generated great income. And that was exactly what they were interested in!

Simply out of greed, they organised a demonstration XIII match between Australia and England at the Pershing Stadium in Paris on 31st December 1933. Not knowing how to address an audience they did not know, they charged Gallia, with his fame, to promote the event. The FFR protested, tried to weakly oppose the match, and then let the matter slide, thinking that nobody would be interested in the match. Big mistake.

Jean Gallia was highly regarded in the community. Hearing him talk about this exceptional forthcoming match drew a crowd of nearly 20,000 into the stands at Pershing Stadium. The commercial success was enormous. The event's sponsors kept the iron hot. Immediately afterwards, the "banished" Toulouse player was asked to put together the first French XIII team, which was going to tour England in March 1934. Gallia would also be deeply involved in the creation of the Ligue Française de Rugby à XIII the following April.

Realising just how wrong its assessment of the situation was, the FFR would never stop trying to reinstate the 5 Nations Championship. This quest was its priority, as it was intended to save the day. In fact, just like the great British transhumance at the end of the 19th century, the number of players in the XV melted like snow in the sun to the benefit of the XIII. Agonising, after losing nearly 30% of its clubs (dissolved or turned to

XIII), the FFR was finally reintegrated into the 5 Nations Championship in 1939, just before the war prevented it from being held until 1947.

Less brutal, more spectacular, and with rules that were easier to understand, thirteen had emerged from the chaos of France to take its place as a sport in its own right. Like their British counterparts, the banned members of French rugby now had a safe haven to call their own.

17.3

The XIII as a counterweight to the XV: in the southern hemisphere

XIII rugby may be the exclusive preserve of Australia, but it was introduced to the southern lands on the initiative of neighbouring New Zealand. Half-pioneers, half-pilgrims, a group of men experienced an epic journey that took them away from home for an entire year. They returned from this journey of initiation as divine messengers, the bearers of a revolutionary rugby, charged with instilling it in their fellow men.

Rugby was introduced under the skies of the Long White Cloud by, as is often the case, the highest social classes. Charles John Monro, son of the future Speaker of the House of Representatives, brought the sport with him. He had been introduced to its codes and customs while studying at Christ's College Finchley in England. Seduced by the values of the game, he managed to convince the teachers at Nelson College to play it at their school. On 12th December 1870, the first rugby match took place in New Zealand. It pitted Nelson College against Wellington.

This game of rugby football was a real treat for the participants. They saw certain aspects of Kī-o-rahi in it, a ball game played by the Maoris and widespread in Aotearoa. The rules were standardised, and rugby slowly spread throughout this vast and sparsely populated territory. The first federation did not appear until ten years later, with the foundation of the Canterbury Rugby Football Union in 1879.

By the time rugby began to take hold in Kiwi territory, this sport was already a long way ahead in neighbouring Australia. Around 1875, local federations already existed, and some regions already had their own championship. Eager to test themselves against other opponents, the Aussies organised the first inter-nations matches, played by clubs or selections during tours. A number of Kiwi clubs, who were just starting out in international rugby, received a visit from a selection of the Australian Southern Rugby Union in 1882. This type of initiative multiplied, fanning the flames of the fervour of the first rugby fans, who only dreamed of glory and travel.

The New Zealand Rugby Union was formed in 1892, bringing together most of the provincial committees. The bodies were ready to register New Zealand's first official match in June 1893 in New South Wales.

There was some disagreement at the beginning of the NZRU's existence. The leaders of the Canterbury province, along with those of Southland and Otago, initially refused to 'submit' to this new central authority. However, the conflict did not last and was settled in the following years. The unrest was just a blip with no consequences. In just a few years, New Zealand managed to establish and perpetuate its national institution.

But rugby was very much on its own in this part of the world, far removed from the rugby 'centre' that was the United Kingdom. Although matches were held regularly, mainly between the southern nations and occasionally against teams from Europe, the repeated confrontations were getting boring. As early as 1902, the NZRU put forward the idea of playing the British nations on their own soil. However, due to a lack of funding, the idea only became a reality a few years later.

On 30th July 1905, 27 Kiwis departed Wellington for England, which they eventually reached after a journey of... 5 weeks!

The tour produced an enormous sporting performance by the New Zealanders. 34 wins out of 35 matches played. They thrashed all their opponents except Wales, who won one match by 3-0. The 'Originals', as they were known, had a reputation for nearly invincibility from their very first European tour. In rugby, that was generally more restrictive than it is today; they won by inflicting huge scores on the unfortunate adversaries who came up against them. One statistic perfectly illustrates this thirst for play and relentless efficiency: the New Zealanders returned home with a total of 59 points conceded, compared to 976 scored! Affixed with a nickname that added to the terror they inspired in their opponents - the All Blacks - their legend was born.

Tens of thousands of spectators flocked to see these aliens from the antipodes, with their fearsome reputation. Their unique playing style, which incorporated bits of Kī-o-rahi, added an exotic touch that captivated the crowds.

The popular enthusiasm generated by its ambassadors enabled the NZRU to make a lucrative financial splash. The total takings from the tour amounted to over £12,000. A fortune at the time! But paradoxically, this financial success, which was not bothered to hide and was even displayed like a trophy, backfired on the New Zealand federation.

At the beginning of the 20th century, the world of New Zealand rugby was not immune to the upheaval surrounding the payment of players' fees. Here, as elsewhere, rugby had to remain a purely amateur sport. But here, as elsewhere, the majority of players were campaigning fervently for 'time off' to be paid and for medical expenses to be covered. In a way, they won their case for the 1905 tour. The NZRU did not use the term 'remuneration' but 'gratification'. The difference lay in the amounts involved...

Indeed, given the length of the tour - almost 8 months - the federation exceptionally agreed to provide financial rewards for its players. But it was taking care to allocate such low sums that, strangely enough, even the RFU had nothing to say about it! It was 3 shillings a day, and not a penny more!

To make thousands of pounds in profit while giving only a handful of shillings to those involved in this success was beyond comprehension. The tour participants felt cheated and made sure they let their officials know. Public opinion was outraged and supported the Originals.

This umpteenth dispute over remuneration only served to fuel the simmering conflict. Those in favour of reasonable (rather than ridiculous) remuneration were pitted against the institutions which advocated purely amateur rugby. In the same way as in the United Kingdom previously and in France later, the federations were creating a breeding ground for the emergence of a dangerous competitor: XIII rugby.

Two figures would emerge from the tumult to become the leaders of the Thirteen-ist pioneers. The first was named George Smith. He took part in the 1905 tour and intimately knew the other Originals, as well as the machinery of the NZRU.

During his stay in England, Smith had the opportunity to attend Northern Rugby Union matches. He enjoyed this kind of maverick rugby, and Smith, far from being solely focused on the sport itself, knew how to count. With a playing style that captivated audiences, each Northern Rugby Union match ensured a substantial return on investment for its organisers. Building on the excellent reputation of the Originals in Europe, George Smith imagined that a new tour of 'Southerners', played according to Northern Union rules, would be a resounding commercial success. He put the idea to James Giltinan, an Australian entrepreneur who was working behind the scenes to develop rugby.

The business tycoon listened attentively and eagerly to the former Original's proposal. The project was seductive and promised huge profits... but remained complex to set up. As a result, although the venture was not abandoned, it remained little more than wishful thinking.

The second character in this fable, Albert Henry Baskerville (also spelt 'Baskiville'), brought the project to life. A skilled organiser, this Wellington Post Office employee and Oriental Club player would embody Smith's imagined tour.

It all began when he accidentally opened a British magazine mislaid in his post office. He came across an article depicting scenes from a recent XIII rugby match played in Bradford. Albert was stunned to learn that the game attracted around 40,000 people. The young man imagined the extraordinary atmosphere that must have reigned in Bradford that day. He imagined all those people gathered there to attend the high mass of a sport whose prophets were still of this world. He guessed the conversations of all those people from all walks of life who came together to share a passion for this fledgling sport. In his reveries, Baskerville found himself transported to the heart of this human tide of jubilant spectators... who had all paid for their tickets! Pragmatic, the young man calculated the profit generated by the event by simple multiplication. And he was speechless. The potential revenue from such a match was considerable!

Baskiville, who was also the author of several rugby books, had no shortage of imagination. He hatched a plan, which started with a daring initiative. He wrote to the Northern Rugby Union, proposing that the British host a touring team from 'Australasia'. In his letter, he argued, as did Smith, that the popularity of XIII rugby in England, combined with the popularity of 'alien' players from Oceania, would ensure the tour's popular and financial success. The Northern Union jumped at the chance and responded favourably and enthusiastically to the proposal. The young postman resigned from his job. He devoted himself full-time to putting together a team from scratch and finding the funding needed to send the whole crew to Europe.

In the greatest secrecy, Albert activated his network. However, few of his contacts were influential enough or trustworthy enough. As for himself, although he had played for Wellington, he only appeared in matches from time to time. He had no particular reputation in local rugby and had the greatest difficulty in the world approaching the best players in the region. It was necessary to acquire the services of a 'representative' who would spearhead the project. A headliner, but a discreet one with a taste for spycraft. The project should not be widely publicised. It was far too early...

This luxury PR man was called George Smith. Perfectly introduced into the milieu, he learned through indiscretions that Baskiville was busy putting together a daring plan. A plan that was exactly the same as the one he and Giltinan had come up with. All the two men needed to do was contribute their address books so that the venture could get off the ground...

Albert and George immediately agreed. The duo complemented each other perfectly. The former was in charge of the stewardship; the latter, who was very popular, made his first recruitments. Baskiville found matches to play in the United Kingdom; Smith, with Giltinan's support, organised events in Australia. The utmost discretion was still the order of the day, and despite the large number of people in the know, the project managed to remain secret for over a year and a half.

In May 1907, a 'leak' appeared in the NZ Herald. A 'possible' professional rugby tour was apparently being planned under the radar. And as the rumour was confirmed, the press unleashed its fury on the expedition. The newspapers fiercely denigrated the initiative, hijacking the name 'All Blacks' to 'All Golds'.

For the oval ball Establishment, this came as a shock. New Zealand's top internationals were about to go on a private tour, playing under Northern Union rules, and all for profit! It sounded so big that the NZRU was not giving the slightest credibility to this venture. Nevertheless, the officials issued a few threats of exclusion for any player taking part in order to dissuade any hesitation they might have had.

Too far from its roots, the federation was unaware that the announcement was, in fact, being welcomed with open arms. Of the 200 players in the inter-provincial championship, 160 applied to Smith! This sudden abundance only made the selection process more difficult. The organisers, therefore, allowed themselves the luxury of tightening up the selection criteria. For example, since the 'new code rugby' was now played with

XIIIs, wing forwards and touch specialists were not included. But beyond their rugby skills, candidates had to be found who were prepared to 'burn the bridges behind them'. Indeed, the risk of being excluded from the XV's federation was hanging over their heads. And finally, the applicant had to have £50 to invest in the tour. Baskiville's idea.

So as not to be accused of professionalism and thus see the tour fail, each member of the expedition was an 'investor' in the expedition itself. Adapted by Baskerville, this clever system was inspired by the organisation of the Australian cricket team's tour in 1902. All the costs would be shared equally by all... as would be the profits! It was a truly mutualist tour.

The group, or should we say the cooperative, was eventually made up of 9 internationals and 14 provincial players. Shortly after their departure, in August 1907, they made their first stop at their Australian neighbours. The Aussies, led by Giltinan, organised themselves in a hurry and created the New South Wales Rugby Football League in the lounges of Sydney's Bateman's Hotel on 8th August 1907. The institution came into being just in time to present the visitors with a selection in a 3-match series. The first XIII rugby match on Australian soil... would not to be! Although it was planned that the two teams would play according to Northern Union rules, there was no copy of these regulations in Australia. So, for once, they would be playing XV rugby!

On the Great Southern Land, the mention of this new code of rugby, which was originally popular and less contact-oriented, aroused curiosity. All the more so, as Smith's promotional tour took place shortly after the outcry raised by the 'Burdon affair'. This Australian XV player broke his collarbone during a match, but the Australian federation remained intransigent. Indifferent to the situation of the unfortunate Alex Burdon, it did not grant him the slightest compensation or reimbursement for his medical treatment. The situation was finally resolved when the top names in sport publicly declared their support for Burdon. In Australia, the same rumours were swirling around players' compensation. Around the world, the scenario was inevitably the same.

When the expedition, reinforced by Dally Messenger (an Australian who had made a strong impression on the organisers), weighted anchor, the missionaries received a dispatch from New Zealand. As expected, the NZRU had decided to ban them for good. There was no way back.

During a stopover in Ceylon, they played a match and reached England at the end of September 1907. The 'Tourists' stationed themselves in Leeds for a fortnight, the time for them to discover the subtleties of XIII and to acclimatise to the weather, which was not as mild as at home.

The New Zealanders easily assimilated the rules of the "new code". Skilled XIII players surprised their hosts by performing well beyond expectations in the first part of their tour. Against the main British clubs, they lost 9 times, drew 2 times and won 17 times. A very promising start for neophytes who had only a few weeks of practice under their belts.

The rest of the campaign proved tougher for the visitors. Unable to compete against regional and national teams, they lost their next 4 matches. Far from being unsettled, they took advantage of these defeats to gain experience that would put them in good standing before the climax of the tour. After another defeat to the Great Britain team, they bounced back to dominate the British in a second match and won the test series by winning their third match 5-8 in Cheltenham.

The British tour thus ended on a very encouraging note. After a final victory over Saint Helens, the New Zealanders packed up and headed home on 29th February 1908. The Kiwis returned to their distant homeland with fewer players than at the start. Some of them, like Duncan McGregor and Jim Gleeson, signed up with Northern English clubs, effective immediately!

The tour was not over, however. The Australians saw the 'All Golds' made another stop on their way home, covered in glory and wealth. Having received divine teaching, they set about, like prophets, to inculcate the rules and customs of 'Northern Union rugby'.

This educational visit fell at just the right time and propelled the New South Wales league, which was in its infancy, to the top of the bill. Newly created by Giltinan, thanks to the profits from the 3 matches played in August 1907, the regional league benefitted from an opportune spotlight. Its popularity was as sudden as it was unexpected. Until 1924 and the creation of the Australian Rugby League Board of Control, the historic NSWRL, together with the Queensland Rugby League, played the role of national federation. These two bodies also took charge of the development of the 'Kangaroos'.

This time, armed with copies of the 'new rugby' guidelines, the New Zealanders organised several XIII rugby demonstration sessions. They then played two matches against a team formed in Newcastle. Wherever the XIII missionaries were passing, crowds were coming in droves. The exhibition matches were a great success, and Newcastle became one of the first bastions of this new rugby. A domestic league was created in 1910. It was a local championship, but one that was nonetheless viable and financially profitable.

5 matches against various regional teams later, the All Golds concluded this initiatory tour with a series of summit tests. Up against them was the Australian XIII team, playing officially for the first time. The hosts were beaten twice but finally saved their honour by winning the final opposition of the tour on 6th June 1908.

This trip, organised from scratch by a handful of men at odds with their own institutions, had an incredible impact. It was a success across the board. The sporting performance was outstanding, and from then on, the southern nations had to be reckoned with on the international XIII rugby scene. In Australia, dissident rugby experienced an exceptional boom and was elevated to the rank of most popular winter sport.

The Northern Rugby Union also took advantage of the event to consolidate its legitimacy. The English 'reformers' thus proved that their young federation was capable of organising international gatherings, just like the 'Fifteen-ists'. Led by talented administrators, these events were financially self-sustaining and even generated profits.

In fact, the Kiwi slingers' tour brought in a total profit of over £5,600, i.e. £300 for each of the daring 'investors'. The tour came to a sad end, however, with the death of one of its creators. On 20th May 1908, at the age of 25, Albert Baskiville passed away in Brisbane Hospital as a result of pneumonia he had contracted shortly before. The genius organiser had no time to finalise his current project: a XIII rugby tour of the United States.

Although this epic adventure contributed greatly to establishing XIII rugby as a major sport in the 'Land Down Under', the repercussions remained limited at first in New Zealand. No man is a prophet in his own country... Indeed, with the scathing attacks on these new code rugby players, the press ended up dumbfounding public opinion, which nevertheless remained in favour of the 'Tourists'. Also, unlike what had happened in Australia, the new rugby was quickly deprived of its best broadcasters. In addition to those who remained in England, others only made a short visit to the country. Nearly half of the participants, including the most symbolic, quickly returned to the United Kingdom, where tempting contracts awaited them. Harold Rowe signed for Leeds, Massa Johnston and Lance Todd left for Wigan, and Edgar Wrigley negotiated a sum of £400 a year in addition to a job as a plumber with the Runcorn club.

Thirteen-a-side rugby had developed everywhere in pure repudiation of the traditionalist system of the XV. By refusing to reconsider its position on the compensation of players, 'original' rugby encouraged the emergence of a sport that directly overshadowed it. Over time, the two institutions lived on either side of a porous boundary, which was crossed in both directions by certain players. In the 1990s, the media, which had already overabundant the XIII with money, turned their ambitions towards the XV. In the end, it was the XIII that imposed its model. And that was undoubtedly the best trick it ever played on its big brother.

17.4
Hypocrisy and sanctions

After the split between football and rugby, and then the spread of rugby, the traditionalist institutions of the 'Home Unions' fought tooth and nail against what they considered to be a degenerative blemish: professionalism. However, since the dawn of rugby, no governing body has managed to chase away the omnipresent spectre of money. While this fight has led to severe sanctions, most of those who had transgressed the rules had slipped through the net. In order to protect their own interests (such as maintaining the number of licence-holders), the federations hypocritically turned a blind eye to the payments done under the table. And despite pretending not to be interested in money, they cleverly filled their cash registers and ensured their own development.

From the earliest days of rugby, a gentlemen's sport, disinterested by its very nature, the RFU's leaders, who idealised the sport too much, came up against the wall of money. To avoid finding themselves administering a shadow federation, they had to compromise their firmly held positions.

The popularity of rugby is heightening local pride. Each club asserted its identity, its playing style and its superiority over other teams. In the past, every town wanted to own the most sumptuous cathedral. Now, towns wanted to impress by building ever more majestic stadiums. British 'club bosses' saw the financial windfall generated by ticket sales and were constantly on the lookout for funds to expand their stadiums. Unable to rely solely on their own resources, they teamed up with private investors, to whom they promised a financial return on the sums loaned. Constrained by these commitments, they had to manage their associations as rigorously as they did their professional activities. They successfully used the same recipes, and it was not long before they were reaping the first profits from rugby.

The key to increasing profits was to maximise stadium occupancy. And to do that, spectators needed to get their money's worth. In order to strengthen their teams and offer a more spectacular performance, the directors of the first clubs came up with the idea of 'importing' talents. They offered the most skilful players the chance to 'take their business elsewhere' in exchange for better-paid jobs. And now that these players were competing, watched by an ever-growing audience, in brand new facilities, it was becoming difficult to argue with them about paying compensation. How could they legitimately make a profit on the backs of the players and at the same time deny them the slightest gratification? Don't forget that they were and still are the main actors in the events.

The RFU, then the IRFB, took up the cause of 'professionalism'. They dissolved clubs and imposed all-out bans, hypocritically forgetting one of their decisions, taken in 1875. That year, shortly after its creation, the RFU decided to reduce the number of players per team from 20 to 15. The aim of this change was to lighten up the game, make it more entertaining and attract more... paying spectators! Generally speaking, all the major national federations had never refused to cash in the slightest penny while imposing famine on their members. Nevertheless, depending on the context, some of them shared a few crumbs of the cake while remaining hidden behind a façade of anti-professionalism.

Despite its intransigence towards its own people, the RFU was one of the first to make an exception. When the Originals visited in 1905, the RFU was well aware that the New Zealanders were being 'gratified' for their participation in the tour. Despite this, the federation did not make a fuss, nor protest or refuse to play the Kiwis. In light of the fantastic sell-out recorded during this tour, it would be a shame to be deprived of such a windfall...

Social unrest broke out in the 1920s and 1930s while British industry suffered. The Welsh Rugby Union saw its best performers, suddenly unemployed, monetised their services by 'going over to the Thirteen-ist enemy'. To stem the exodus, Welsh officials, even though they were founding members of the International Board, approached the government. They obtain rugby men to be recruited by a force that was not in a state of crisis at the time: the police! As well as bolstering their ranks, the police force was hoping to become acceptable again. By recruiting these sportsmen, who had the full support of the public, the police were trying to make up for the overzealous reprimands they had given to striking workers.

In other times, in other places, while South Africa was isolated politically and in terms of rugby, few cared about what went on in the bowels of the South African Rugby Board. Star fly-half Naas Botha 'confessed' to receiving a fee for every match he played for the Northern Transvaal in the 1980s. 'Don't forget that we were paid ZAR 5!' he said with some amusement. To put that sum into perspective, in Botha's playing days, one could buy a dozen chocolate bars at the corner shop for that amount. Should a handful of Mars and Snickers bars be considered 'payment', or did that fall into a grey area?

The same Naas Botha had never ceased to strive for professional rugby. Money had always been a factor in his sporting choices. 'Other people have made money from their talents. Why should a businessman have the right to be paid for his work? I had sporting talent. Why wasn't I entitled to earn money from my talent?'

While some of the 'payments' were somewhat laughable, and everything else remained under the close scrutiny of the IRFB, it had a territory of relative freedom. A 'salary haven for rugby men'; a jurisdiction that interpreted in its own way the rules laid down by its intimate English enemy: France! From the very beginnings of rugby, these irreverent Latins institutionalised a system of compensation in plain sight. The FFR had never really 'got its hands dirty' in this respect unless forced to do so by the IRFB or the RFU. The French had always been content to sit back and smooth things over while shamelessly practising the famous brown amateurism.

In the hexagonal country, rugby is a subject of passion, heightening local rivalries. In some areas, whole sections of society live and dream through their favourite clubs. Defeat is no longer the loss of a team but of a village or town. In such conditions, respect for amateurism was of secondary importance. In France, more than anywhere else, money was at the centre of the debate.

In 1930, twelve clubs decided to split from the FFR. Their aim was to protest against the violence endemic to rugby, as well as recent evidence of professionalism. In their letter of grievance to their federation, these 'romantics' did not forget to point out that they would only 'return to order' once the financial equalisation system was abolished. Because yes, at that point, revenues were pooled and then distributed. These partisans of 'purely amateur' rugby felt aggrieved by the shortfall imposed by the sharing of the spoils. Far from their utopian image, they were not as disinterested as they claimed.

In the wake of this upheaval, France was excluded from the 5 Nations Championship in 1931 for violence and acts of professionalism. It was not until the end of the Second World War that France was reinstated in the Tournament after the resounding punishment of some of those who had been martyred as an example to others.

Following its 'sweep' in the early 1930s, the FFR pleaded with the IRFB for its reinstatement in the 5 Nations Championship. Its pleas went unheard. The request was rejected. The Dubliners justified this rejection by citing the case of US Quillan, which was a far too blatant example of brazen professionalism.

In the late 1920s, this small village in the foothills of the Pyrenees had a population of around 3,000. Many were making their living, directly or indirectly, from a hat factory run by Jean Bourrel. The businessman also controlled the village rugby club. He had a plan in mind and revealed it openly, without bluntness or tongue-in-cheek: 'I'm sure I'll get more commercial exposure by putting together a team to win the French championship than by putting up posters around the region.'

By promoting the 'purity of the air in his village', patron Bourrel was building his team. And he did it rather well. He equipped it with a physiotherapist and the first doctors specialising in nutrition, and he capitalised on a major advantage: its proximity to Perpignan, whose club was French champion in 1925. With an abundance of arrangements, Bourrel 'offered' his village a team that included up to 7 former Perpignan players and no less than 7 internationals.

US Quillan, a small local club, suddenly became a three-time finalists in the French championship. In 1928, 1929 and 1930, Quillan went from strength to strength, challenging prestigious rivals. In 1929, the club even won the French championship, much to the pride of Bourrel, who promptly... abandoned the ship! Having achieved the notoriety he had hoped for, the hatter decided to cut off supplies in 1930: 'I decided to limit the costs involved in maintaining our team'. Deprived of funding, US Quillan fell back into anonymity.

In 1952, just a few years after returning to the 5 Nations Championship, France was once again threatened with exclusion. Again, for the same reasons: brown amateurism. The FFR, which had learnt the lesson of 1931, wanted to avoid such a sanction at all costs, as it would slow down its expansion. The French federation, therefore, complied with the requirements of the IRFB, which expected exemplary punishment. The French provided the Board with a list of players, others 'sacrificed', suspected of professionalism or 'guilty' of playing XIII. By serving up the heads of a handful of guilty parties on a platter, the FFR managed to save its skin. It even promised to dissolve its championship, which was still held responsible for the violence that continued to plague its stadiums.

Having shown its credentials, the FFR was going about its day-to-day affairs, forgetting its fine promises. Business as usual! The championship would never be disbanded; the very idea would never be raised again. As for disguised professionalism, it had changed, and the methods for avoiding being caught were becoming more complex. Clubs, through their partners, were now investing in rugby players who wanted to set up a business. By 'liberalising' its rugby and giving it an attractive framework, France charmed a few heavyweights. For example, it was by using this kind of 'helping hand' that the small club of Saint Claude succeeded in recruiting foreign internationals.

So, in 1980, while playing in the second division, the Blue and Whites secured the services of Nigel Horton, a former England lock, as a player-coach. When he left the Jura, he was replaced by another international, Nick Mallett, who had two caps for the Springboks. The native of England, who grew up in Rhodesia, settled in Saint Claude in 1985. It was his fellow countryman, Dugald MacDonald, also an international, who 'put him on the spot': 'Dugald told me that the job came with an opportunity to run your own business, Café le Club, which was a small bar and bistro. All the profits would go to me, and when Dugald gave me the figures, it was far more than I was earning in South Africa.'

Replacing Horton as player-coach, Mallett also took over the bar. However, the two English-speaking men were able to carry out their mission successfully, and the Jura club reached the first division by the end of the 1980s. As for the two men, they officially earned no income from rugby...

At the same period, a little further south-east, the Italian championship was also making headlines by attracting the services of some of rugby's greatest names. It was still hard to believe that these players travelled to the other side of the world every year, on their own dime, to play for Italian clubs for free, simply because they loved the Dolce Vita.

Between 1984 and 1993, the legend David Campese, then at the peak of his career, won the Italian championship 5 times with Petrarca Padova and Amatori Rugby Milano. Benetton Treviso hooked up with All Black wingers Craig Green (1987-1991) and John Kirwan (1986-1990). Rovigo snapped up international back row forward Nick Mallett (before his Jura adventure) and, above all, Naas Botha between 1987 and 1993. The South African number 10's views on professional rugby were already well known. The rumours of lucrative contracts disguised as jobs with sponsor companies took on their full meaning.

Far from speculating, Emile N'Tamack, after his career came to an end, openly confirmed that brown amateurism was institutionalised in France: 'Before 1995, we were already earning a bit of money from rugby, but it wasn't our main activity, it was a bonus. We simply shook hands with our presidents; nothing was contractual or official, and it worked more with match bonuses.' There you have it.

The second World Cup was held in 1991. According to the IRFB, doubts about whether it would be held were quickly swept aside by the success of the 1987 edition. Since that event, the rugby union has grown in popularity. However, national federations noticed an exponential growth in their revenues. By 'success', the International Board no doubt meant 'financial'.

From the first bets organised by English bookmakers at the end of the 19th century to the windfalls collected by the federations, money has always been present around, if not in, the universe of rugby. But until 1995, simply saying its name was a dirty word. 'We do these things, but we don't say so'. And everyone only sees what everyone agrees to see.

Nevertheless, by trying too hard to regulate their world without getting to know it in depth, the traditionalist organisations, the guardians of the original spirit of Rugger, became very close to breaking up. The deflagration caused by the switch to professionalism in 1995, which forced them to face reality. By opening their eyes to the real situation, the officials soon realised that the principle of amateurism, erected as a dogma, was nothing but an illusion.

17.5
1995: The change, please!

It was 18th December 2014, 8.30 am. The press had been invited to the Racing Metro 92 training centre in Plessis-Robinson. The Parisian directors had an announcement to make. They wanted to publicly unveil, a week ahead of time, the lovely Christmas present their club gave itself.

In front of an audience of journalists, a giant screen lifted up. The cheerful face of Dan Carter appears. The All Blacks fly-half, a star if ever there was one, one of rugby's greats, announced that he joined the ranks of Racing Metro 92. He would not arrive straight away but in a year's time! Nevertheless, the deal was already sealed, and the New Zealand genius looked forward to honouring it. And for good reason, this contract was one of the most important. Jacky Lorenzetti, the chairman of the Parisian club, revealed that Dan Carter had been offered an 'annual salary of close to €1.1 million'.

How did we go from players being excluded because of a handful of shillings or a job as a foreman to players becoming millionaires in Euros in just one season? Have we changed the dimensions? Is it a dream? No. Far from the world of dreams, rugby union had, in reality, collided head-on with a force that far surpasses its ideals: sponsorship and media money!

Since its creation, XV rugby has officially remained a purely amateur sport. In the British Isles, many cases of professionalism, also known as brown amateurism, led to the banishment of the offenders. In contradiction to this doctrine of amateurism, XIII rugby developed as an alternative to the XV. Through a play of mirrors, this 'false brother' of the Thirteen put unbearable financial pressure on the XV's institutions. In the mid-1990s, the century-old International Rugby Football Board was forced to return to its emblematic principle: amateurism.

The revolution came in 1995, the year the IRFB agreed to lose a round of multi-cushion billiards so as not to lose the game.

France, the first non-British nation to join the IRFB in 1978, had long campaigned for the organisation of a World Cup. The Board, in open opposition, described the idea as 'far-fetched' and sought to stifle it. Rugby's world governing body put the brakes on. Above all, it feared initiating the slightest movement that could open the door to professionalisation. It was for the same reasons that no club from across the UK took part in an attempt at a European Club Cup in the 1960s.

At the beginning of the 1980s, the FFR and its president, Albert Ferrasse, found federations on the Board that supported its proposals. Australia and New Zealand, who had nothing but tours to shine on the international stage, were also keen to see the creation of a world tournament.

At the same moment, in Australia, David Lord was a popular sports journalist. He was a specialist in rugby league, broadcasting on Channel 9, among other channels. In 1983, he put forward a serious project for XV rugby, based around the creation of a world club league, incorporating the best players in the world and leading to a world cup for national teams.

As in the case of XIII, all costs would be covered by image rights and sponsorship. As for the profits, it would be up to the entities created to share them with the players.

At the mention of this last parameter, the ears of the latter perked up. The proposal, which, it seemed, was no joke, was of the utmost interest to them. Indeed, much to their chagrin, the players were more than ever excluded from sharing in the gold pot that was constantly growing. Clubs, provinces and federations were gorging themselves while refusing to give the slightest crumb to the players, without whom nothing would be possible. It was against this backdrop that nearly 200 of them, including several internationals, secretly signed up with David Lord and his emissaries.

When the project was revealed, the IRFB was taken literally by storm. Surprised to learn that several hundred players had already agreed in principle to play under other flags, the Board could only promise sanctions to those who took the plunge... or who got too close to the Australian journalist.

The Lord project remained a threat that hung over the IRFB's head for almost two years. If the idea was definitively abandoned in the face of threats of reprisals, the federations came very close to imploding. They had no choice but to reconsider organising a World Cup. Not that everyone agreed, but they knew that if they didn't do it, others would! The wake-up call had seriously shaken the various organisations. They realised the extent to which their almighty power could suddenly be threatened by proposals from 'elsewhere'. Driven by different ideals and interests, the outside world had no use for their rules and codes of conduct.

The officials also realised how much they depend on the players. They were the ones that the crowds enjoyed watching. They were the ones who made young and old dream. They were the stars of the entertainment. However, the showmen seemed ready to let them down for any reasonable financial offer.

Forced into action, the IRFB members met in Paris in March 1985 and examined the idea of creating a World Cup. It was fairly assumed that the vote would be a draw. The four Home Unions would remain united in the 'no' vote, while Australia, New Zealand, France and South Africa would support the 'yes' vote. The Springboks representatives, although their nation was sidelined from world rugby, had nevertheless retained their voting rights.

The surprise came from the English and Welsh. Against all expectations, their representatives were revising their positions during the council meeting. The creation of the World Cup was approved! The organisation was entrusted to Australia and New Zealand. As for the date, it was set for May and June 1987.

The IRFB was putting out the fire while skilfully casting a discreet veil over the second aspect of the Lord project, which was player remuneration.

The success of the first World Cup prompted the IRFB to repeat the experiment, and the enthusiasm generated by the second, in 1991, sent a whiff of money up the media manias. Among them was the Australian Rupert Murdoch. With his *News Corporation*, he was already heavily involved in the Rugby League, a popular championship on the Great Southern Land, which generated extraordinary earnings for the media conglomerate.

The businessman knew well that the situation was explosive for XV rugby, particularly in his own country. Thirteen-ist clubs and federations were becoming increasingly pressing. With the backing of professional status, generous contracts and rights to broadcast, the Australian and New Zealand XIII was in the process of devouring its big brother, the XV, and draining it of its marrow. The players, nervous and on edge, wanted more than ever, and rightly so, to get their share of the profits. Many had already received substantial offers to move to XIII. The kind of offer no one turns down! Agreements in principle were concluded, and contracts were due to be finalised after the 1995 World Cup.

The Australian federation, already in its death throes, knew that without rapid and radical change, it would suffer a bleeding of talents. The IRFB was keeping a close eye on the Australian situation, fearing, above all, that contagion would spread to the rest of the rugby world. Like the International Board, Murdoch was on the lookout and patiently biding his time.

On 8th April 1995, in a last-chance meeting, the main decision-makers in southern rugby gathered. The stakes were high: to prevent the best players from leaving to play XIII rugby. Everyone knew that good words and general rounds of drinks wouldn't be enough. They needed to be paid. And not just any old way, since the proposal was to match, no more and no less, the salaries offered by the XIII Super League.

With its finances in dire straits, the Australian association had no choice but to approach the media... including the *News Corporation*! Just the thing, Murdoch had a number of projects waiting in the pipeline.

In order to administer television rights and various other common interests, the 3 major nations of the South grouped together to form

SANZAR. The mission of this newly-created SANZAR was to help Murdoch develop other competitions and to finalise the partnership project with *News Corporation* before the end of the World Cup. The young institution was also responsible for initiating discussions with the players in order to negotiate their first salaries. They waited for this for so long; they would be over the moon! Once again, the officials were running a little late.

In the shadows, other sharp fangs gleamed. Those of a powerful Constrictor who had already begun to clamp down on his prey. Kerry Packer, who ran a powerful Australian media consortium, had been drooling over the rights to XV rugby for a very long time. His group already owned some of the TV rights to the XIII Super League, and its influential leader was interested in XV rugby, which he considered more universal. Like Murdoch, he was perfectly aware of the turbulence in the world of the Fifteen-ists.

Having already snapped up the broadcasting rights to cricket in the late 1970s, Kerry knew the recipe for making a previously amateur sport attractive and bankable. The difficulty for him was to secure the cooperation of the Fifteen's leaders. As they were already in talks with his fiercest competitor, it would not be possible to approach them directly.

Packer brought back the Lord project from the 1980s and dusted it off. The chairman of *9 Network* decided to take a different tack. He initiated a strategy of change from the bottom up. Through the intermediary of the players, those who created the show, Packer wanted to twist the arm of the federations.

Sensing that rugby union was ready to be plucked like low-hanging fruit, he appointed Geoff Levy, and Ross Turnbull, a former Wallaby turned lawyer, to initiate talks with the players. Their prerogative was to secure their commitments by contract. These contracts, backed by substantial sponsorship deals, were lucrative, it goes without saying.

Under the direction of their big boss, Levy and Turnbull created the World Rugby Corporation, the entity that would officially oversee the 'Packer system'. The 3 Australians had no shortage of imagination and were thinking big. Through the WRC, they would not only try to control Southern rugby; with millions of dollars, they were planning to compete with the IRFB by getting their hands on the nuggets of XV rugby and then setting up competitions that would make them shine... and at the same time, generate handsome returns on their investments.

Turnbull imagined a concept with several 'drawers' featuring 3 separate conferences of 10 teams drawn from all over the globe. The best players would be selected to create provinces, which would meet in a global tournament. At the top of this pyramid of talents, national teams, incorporating the cream of the crop of players, would compete in a World Cup.

Murdoch's task was facilitated by direct contact with the federations. Levy and Turnbull, on the other hand, were working like ants. Just as David Lord had done ten years earlier, they canvassed, one by one, in the greatest secrecy, each of the potential participants in this project. Armed with their pilgrim's staff, they met with players and sponsors (including *ESPN* in the United States), who were unanimously won over by this shake-up of organisations and signed up to the RWC.

In pursuit of their goal of a worldwide system, Packer's envoys spread out across the globe. Before the World Cup, they exposed their plans to the top brass of Northern rugby, gathered in London. The audience was thrilled by the pitch, and new engagements were signed immediately.

However, to avoid being thwarted, the plan had to remain secret for as long as possible. The 'conspirators' only planned to come out of the woodwork after the World Cup. The South African World Cup was, therefore, the deadline for the two competing projects. By taking advantage of the extraordinary leverage provided by the players' engagements, Packer found himself on the verge of winning his race for TV rights against Rupert Murdoch!

For the first time, the balance of power between the players and their federations was completely reversed, thanks to the support provided by the WRC's money. Turnbull and Levy were working tirelessly and continued to rack up the commitments. They couldn't afford to slack off, as they needed to collect almost 900 signatures to ensure that the teams in the 3 conferences had enough people!

On 24th June, the date of the World Cup final, a bombshell was released! SANZAR announced that it had signed an exclusive television rights contract with *News Corporation*. The amount was staggering at the time; as agreed, it was about 55 million US dollars per season!

The Packer team dealt a huge blow, having just seen pulled the rug out from under. But there was still hope! The commitment was sealed only for the three major nations of the South. The door to the northern teams remained open. And then, contractually, it was with the WRC that the best were engaged. Emptied of its substance, this championship, admittedly broadcasted by Murdoch, would not be worth much...

These top players, who were the focus of all the negotiations, were not at all pleased that their federations had negotiated stratospheric sums with advertisers without even being consulted. They had the impression that they were nothing but merchandise and were losing a lot in the Murdoch project! When the SANZAR representatives approached the players to offer them their first professional contracts, they were left dubious about their reactions. After campaigning, sometimes brazenly, to improve their situation, they turned up their noses at the offers. And reject them! SANZAR didn't get it... it came back at them, proposing 'extras' with the same effect. It was enough to make you lose your marbles!

At this point, the inter-federations organisation was still unaware of the existence of the WRC project. Behind the scenes, the WRC project continued to gain credibility, offering salaries up to 3 times higher than those of SANZAR! After numerous attempts of contact, the 'southern' body was starting to feel the cold sweat. The Super 12 and Tri-Series had already been scheduled but were in danger of becoming empty shells if no player committed...

Officials from the southern nations soon understood the reasons for their difficulties. In July 1995, the content of the 'rival' negotiations leaked to the press. Down with the masks! They fell off their chairs as they read interviews with some of the biggest names in the game, who had already signed up with the WRC or were about to do so. And indeed, the salary proposals had nothing to do with those of SANZAR.

On 28th July, the day before a Bledisloe Cup match, further revelations about the functioning of the WRC, skilfully elaborated by Levy and Turnbill, appeared in the newspapers. What was thought to be an epiphenomenon was about to gather enough participants to crush all other projects. Professionalisation was inevitable. And it was just around the corner. It remained to be seen which route it would take. In the summer of 1995, a number of players were overwhelmed by offers from both the WRC and SANZAR, not to mention those from XIII rugby, which was always on the lookout for opportunities. Would rugby in the southern hemisphere survive the implosion?

Murdoch was also flabbergasted when he realised that SANZAR had signed up his companies without having locked in the players' participation. Furious, he ordered the body to match any offer, whether it came from WRC, Thirteen or anything else. But the seduction operation was still not working. The main players seemed to have opted for emancipation. At the end of August, WRC announced that 400 of them had already signed up. Pressured by Murdoch and *his News Corporation*, SANZAR was totally upside down.

If the carrot they dangled was not enough to convince, then the institutions would use the stick. The recalcitrant players were destabilised; there was talk of permanent banishment... Charismatic personalities and popular former New Zealand and Australian players preached for the federal parish. In South Africa, the voice of SARU was relayed by Kitch Christie, fresh from his World Cup title. He urged the players to sign with their federations: 'for the team, for the country, for yourself and for what you have achieved'.

Criticised by serious and influential opponents, the WRC project was beginning to falter. No one was committing themselves anymore, while others were backing down. The edifice, not yet complete, teetered on the brink of collapse. Rupert won his fight against Kerry. Willy-nilly, the players fell into line.

In Europe, in the torpor of summer, the IRFB and the European nations were suddenly awakened by turmoil in the southern hemisphere. For the second time in this story, the masks came off. The Home Unions were shocked to find out what had been going on away from home. They discovered that most of the discussions had taken place behind closed doors, without anyone knowing. A real conspiracy! But given the sums of money involved, SANZAR did everything in its power to ensure that the deal went through and dispensed with any authorisation to act.

With its back to the wall, taken completely by surprise, the IRFB immediately gauged the consequences of the transition to professionalism in the three major countries of the South. In the space of a few years, they would gain such a technical and physical lead that the European nations would remain second fiddle forever. In reaction to this news, which had the effect of an earthquake, the IRFB convened an emergency council for 3 days, from 24 to 26th August. The outcome of the meeting, held at the Ambassador Hotel in Paris, left little room for doubt. Major changes were made. The statements made by Vernon Pugh, Chairman of the Board, all pointed in this direction: 'Whether we like it or not, rugby will become professional in a very short space of time. If we don't anticipate that change, lead it and control it, the IRB and the federations, as we know them today, are in danger of becoming completely out of control.'

The Board gave in. In a new speech, Vernon Pugh declared that rugby was now an 'open' sport. The measure was a significant one. Rugby was officially authorised to become a professional sport; players could now devote themselves solely to playing the game and monetise their talents. To avoid being rendered obsolete and possibly disappearing, the IRB debunked its anti-professional stance and rendered invalid one of its flagship rules, established in 1893.

Journalist Peter Jackson was in Paris that day. He recalls: 'It was clear that rugby was going to become professional, or at least be "open" so that it could move forward. But none of us really thought the Board would have the courage to go through with it and, to their credit, even belatedly, they did it in one fell swoop.'

In the end, the oldest and most influential organisation found itself forced, through a backlash, to accept what it had always refused. Media money was far too powerful an adversary, even for them. And what can be said about the Rugby Leagues, which took great pleasure in constantly dangling meteoric contracts in the face of disillusioned XV stars? As far back as the 1980s, the legendary David Campese was constantly approached by 13-a-side clubs. He turned down all their offers, including one from Saint Helens RFS for £300,000 for 3 years!

As soon as this new market opened up, everyone rushed in and stuffed their faces. Mike Catt became the first player in the Northern Hemisphere to turn 100% professional. In France in 1996, 600 players signed their first professional contracts. The average salary amounts to 6,000 Francs (around €1,000), with the highest salary peaking at 70,000 Francs (around €11,000). In the 1998/99 Championship, the average budget per club was €3 million. In 2018/19, it was already 30 million. Inflation was considerable. The sums will continue to rise, and the transfer prices of the stars of the game will set new records every season. When compared with the 3 shillings a day earned by the Originals in 1905 with Dan Carter's million Euros a year, it's clear that professional rugby came a long way...

18

The Argentinian Bajadita

The Bajadita is an eight-man push technique devised in Argentina in the 1970s. This method, which made the Albiceleste pack one of the most feared in the world, served as the basis for current techniques. It is Argentina's legacy in world rugby.

The Bajadita was modelling in the mid-1960s in the mind of Izaac van Heerden, a South African. He was sent to Argentina by his federation to help the local national team (not yet known as the Pumas) prepare for a tour. Van Heerden used this trip to try out his collective push method with great success. The technique was then adopted and improved by Fransisco Ocampo, the coach of the San Isidoro Club in Buenos Aires. Once its effectiveness had been proven, this innovative technique would gradually spread throughout Argentina and then the rest of the world, revolutionising, among other things, the players' positions in the scrum.

OK, but there aren't 6 ways of pushing, so what's the secret? Actually, it's a series of postures and bounds, the main aim of which is to put maximum pressure on the opposing right prop and to use the hooker as a third prop.

Until that time, the left prop engaged the scrum with his left foot forward. Under pressure, his hips tended to drop outwards. As a result, the lock's thrust lost much of its effectiveness, and a weak point was created on the left prop's inside shoulder. This gave the opposing right prop every opportunity to push slightly across the gap or to push straight at the hooker.

With the Bajadita, the three front row players attack the scrum with their feet on the same line. In addition, the left prop positions his shoulder under the armpit of his hooker. As a consequence, the left-hand prop can't drop back, there's no weak point on his inside shoulder and the second row can push forward with full effect. Added to this is a much lower position, very much stretched out, which makes better use of the power of the lower limbs. Finally, the second row does not link up with the props between the legs but on their outside hips to tighten up the front row.

Often, the hooker doesn't even bother to heel. By gaining ground on impact, the ball goes straight down the lane. This way, with both legs firmly planted on the floor, he can bring extra power to the push.

When the Argentinians first used this technique in international matches, the opposing backs found themselves completely devoid of solutions. Jean-Pierre Garuet, who encountered the Argentinian pack in 1986, declares that "it was a wall! A compact mass against which we could do nothing!"

Jacques Fouroux, who was coaching the French national team during their tour of the southern hemisphere in 1986, tried his utmost to decipher the Argentine pushing technique. He would later test a variation of it in the early 1990s with his pack of *Mammoths* from Grenoble. Other French coaches would soon follow suit. At the same time, other clubs and national teams around the world were also inspired by this method. Given its effectiveness, all packs will end up using positions more or less similar to those of the Bajadita. The modern scrum was born…

19

The extraordinary life of Mr Mayor

To be crowned French rugby champion for 3 consecutive seasons is an honourable achievement. However, these 3 titles, won in 1922, 1923 and 1924 by Marcel-Frédéric Lubin-Lebrère, could almost be described as details in a life that combines rugby, the Great War and incredible situations.

Born in Agen in 1891, Lubin-Lebrère settled in Toulouse in 1913. He joined the Stade Toulousain, where he played as a prop or lock. His imposing size and sturdiness for the time earned him his first three caps for the French national team in 1914, during the 5 Nations Championship. He scored his first try for Les Bleus in his 3rd cap against England. That year, Scotland declined to play France. The two teams would share the wooden spoon, an imaginary anti-trophy awarded to teams that lost every match in the tournament.

The First World War also broke out in 1914. Marcel-Frédéric was called up for military service like so many others, and after the mud of the rugby pitches, he would have to join the muddy trenches. The Great War, with all its horrors, would shatter the destinies of millions of people;

paradoxically, it would also make the destiny of the Toulouse player outstanding.

The native of the French Southwest took part in the dreadful Battle of the Somme with his unit in 1916. After an assault on enemy positions, his comrades did not see him returning to his barracks. He was reported missing and was declared by the military authorities to have been killed in action.

Lubin-Lebrère actually had a thick skin. To everyone's amazement, he made a comeback in 1919 on the Ponts-Jumeaux pitch, the home of Stade Toulousain, almost three years after his official demise.

What happened to the rugby player during those three years? It was the man himself who would tell it best, on numerous occasions, in a narrative that was always highly colourful. During that Somme offensive, a grenade exploded near him. Wounded in the eye, he lost the use of it for good and lay groggy on the battlefield for several hours. Afterwards: "I woke up. I was between the two lines and had lost a lot of blood. I said to myself: Lubin, you can't stay here. I lift myself up... and I take a bullet in the... I fall again [...] I stand up. Bang! Another bullet catches me. I tried four times, but each time I took a bullet, except the last time when the guy who was aiming at me used a machine gun and put twelve in my body!"

Spotted and unable to move, Marcel-Frédéric was taken by a German patrol. He was taken prisoner and treated by his enemies, who removed the bullets they had riddled him with (various sources mention a different total of bullets, ranging from 11 to 17). Liberated at the end of hostilities, he was able to return to Toulouse, where he laced up his rugby boots again shortly afterwards.

1919 was also the year when the rugby authorities decided that sport must take precedence over the trauma of the Great War. On 1st January 1920, the 5 Nations Championship opened in Paris with a match between France and Scotland. The squads of the two teams, decimated at the front by four years of hostilities, were largely renewed (125 international rugby players from all nations perished in the mud of the trenches).

That day, Lubin-Lebrère was invited back to wear the blue jersey, tasked with being one of the leaders of this new team, which included 11 new players. France fell to a 5-0 defeat, but the scoreline was a mere detail. The focus shifted to another aspect of the game, which would come to be known as the one-eyed match. Lubin-Lebrère, Thierry - on the French side - Hume, Laing and Wemyss - on the Scottish side - all lost an eye in the Great War!

On 31st January, the French XV travelled to England to take on the Red Roses Team. The match ended in another French loss, 8-3. At the post-match reception at Twickenham, the English officials were taken aback to hear Lubin-Lebrère being called *Monsieur le Maire (Mister Mayor)* by his team-mates. The nickname was simply given to him because he was a civil servant at the town hall. But the English didn't know that. One of them ventures to ask him which town he was the mayor of. Without flinching, the Frenchman naturally replies: "Toulouse!". As a result, he was introduced as such to all those gathered that evening and was seated at the table alongside the king's representatives! (Some sources mention that this anecdote occurred during a trip to Scotland).

The 1920 5 Nations Championship concluded with France travelling to Ireland. The players from the French national team arrived in Dublin, which was on fire, almost under a state of siege, in the midst of the Irish

War of Independence. Les Bleus received a rude welcome from the Dublin rabble. On the way to their hotel, they suddenly found themselves surrounded by a hostile mob wielding clubs. The situation seemed intractable and on the verge of degenerating. It was at this point that Lubin-Lebrère boldly, but very simply, launched into the crowd in his gravelly voice: "French Team! French Team!" As if magnetised, the crowd quietened down and moved aside to let the players head to their hotel.

Charles Brennus, the famous man accompanying the French team, recounted that during the same trip, Marcel-Frédéric mysteriously vanished into thin air. Worried, all the members of the group set out to find him, but to no avail. It was only a few hours later that they were summoned to come and collect the player... from the police station!

While strolling through the streets of Dublin, the Toulousan heard a familiar tune, *La Marseillaise*, rising from a cellar. He joined the improvised choir and enthusiastically sang his national anthem, unaware that it had also been adopted by the independence fighters and recognised as a revolutionary song! Shortly afterwards, a police patrol burst into the premises and arrested everyone present. Lubin-Lebrère's enthusiasm led to him being suspected of belonging to the Irish separatist movement for a few hours.

After all these twists and turns, the episode of this Irish tour would have a happy and historic epilogue: the first victory of the French XV outside France.

In 1921, Lubin-Lubrère's Stade Toulousain failed to win the French championship in the final, losing 5-0 to Perpignan. With a vengeance, the Pink City's XV, of which Monsieur le Maire was a member, will go on to win the next successive three titles, in 1922, 1923 and 1924.

The Toulousan survivor also captured a silver medal with the Olympic rugby team at the 1924 games. Once again, the small history merges with the big. Of course, Marcel-Frédéric, by now a master in the art of finding himself in unpredictable situations, was in on the act!

France met the United States in the Olympic rugby final on 18th May 1924. There were only 3 participants in the tournament, with Romania as the third nation. Convinced of their superiority and praised by the press, the French received a real cold shower when they lost 17-3. The match turned into a real brawl. It was the scene of a terrible outburst of violence, both on and off the pitch. Some of the 20,000 spectators present that day were also coming to blows in the stands. The French fans, vexed and furious at the beating they had received, violently lashed out at anyone sympathetic to the opposing team.

The match and the incidents surrounding it were qualified at the time as "the best that can be done without knives or guns". The Olympic Committee would decide to withdraw rugby from the Games. The veil was cast over the Olympic oval ball until 2016 when rugby sevens returned to the Games - an absence of 92 years!

Marcel-Frédéric Lubin-Lebrère, after living through so many moments that marked history in general and rugby in particular, retired from international rugby in 1925 during the 5 Nations Championship. He went on to wear the cockerel jersey on 15 occasions.

After that, he continued to play for Stade Toulousain, but gradually gave way to the younger generation, playing only in the second or third team. After hanging up his boots for good, he coached his lifelong club in 1927 and 1928. "He remained a manager until his death. He attended all the training sessions. He was a true Toulousan, straightforward and upright," said Henri Fourès.

Marcel-Frédéric Lubin-Lebrère died in July 1972 at the age of 80, at the end of a life full of mischief, during which he came close to death and played a part in moments that have remained engraved in popular memory. His battered body now rests in peace, while his soul has undoubtedly returned to the paradise of warriors... unless it has joined the Eden of pranksters.

20

1974: The first official streaker

On 20th April 1974, Twickenham Stadium was buzzing. The sworn enemy, France, had crossed the Channel to take on the Red Roses. This friendly, or should we say charity match, had no sporting stakes whatsoever.

When the half-time whistle blew, the journalists and photographers left their "stands" to stretch their legs. As for the spectators, they rushed to the various refreshment stands to "refuel" before the beginning of the second half.

On this day, unusually, the players were taking shelter in the changing rooms for the break. And as the last of the stragglers made their way into the tunnel, a clamour erupted from the stands. An unusual din peppered with laughter and booing.

Ian Bradshaw, a freelance photographer for the Sunday Mirror, was present at Twickenham that day. His mission was to catch the best images of the match.

Unlike his colleagues, who have gone to the stadium tunnel in search of the warmth of a cup of tea, Ian remained at his station during half-time. He was situated in the front row, as close to the pitch as possible, in the south corner.

When the amused roar of the crowd grew louder, the photographer, puzzled, surveyed the stadium to find the cause. The spectacle he witnessed had never been seen before in a sports stadium. He arms his Nikkormat and immortalised the moment. He didn't know it yet, but his photo would go around the world.

※

The last time France and England met was just a few weeks ago. In the heart of winter 1974, in Paris, the two teams were facing off in the 5 Nations Championnat. It was the first time that the Parc des Princes was hosting the traditional "Crunch", which ends in a 12-12 draw. But the result would quickly be overshadowed by another, far more dramatic, event.

The next day - 3rd March - at half past noon, a Turkish Airlines DC-10 flew from Istanbul to London via Paris and skidded off the Paris runway at Orly en route to Heathrow. Less than ten minutes after take-off, the cockpit received a high-priority alarm. The cargo hold was no longer pressurised. And with good reason: the door to the hold had ripped off, taking part of the aircraft's fuselage with it.

At precisely 12:41 minutes and 13 seconds, as the aircraft in difficulty was hurtling towards the ground at a speed of around 700 km/h, it disappeared from the control screens. The wreckage of flight 981 would be found shortly afterwards near Meaux, in the Ermenonville forest.

The impact on the ground was terrible, leaving no chance for the 346 occupants of the DC-10. There were no survivors. Among the 335 passengers were 18 players and English club Bury St Edmonds Rugby Club supporters who had come to watch the previous day's match. The emotion caused by their loss, as well as by this massive air disaster, prompted the French and English national teams to organise a charity match to raise funds. This friendly match was scheduled for 20th April at Twickenham.

On the D-day , As he often did, Ian Bradshaw took up position behind the south goal line, between the first row of spectators and the in-goal. He particularly liked this perspective, which allowed him to cover more of the pitch and capture the movements in full view.

Michael O'Brien, a young Australian accountant based in London, was still anonymous at this time of the afternoon. A keen rugby fan, he and his friends were also at Twickenham on Saturday.

Kick-off was at 3 pm. The spring sun was shining, but it had a hard time warming the atmosphere. Michael, like many others, crowded into the refreshment bars to enjoy the fairground atmosphere. There was nothing like it to cheer you up and raise your body temperature a few degrees!

As kick-off approached, the Australian and his group of friends took their seats and continued to hydrate themselves copiously. Imbued, the young men asked themselves, amused: "Would it be possible for someone to walk across the field completely naked?"

Still joking, one of O'Brien's English comrades challenged him to answer this question by checking for himself. "Don't bet with O'Brien because he'll do it," warned the others. But the young accountant was still sober enough and refused the bet.

The first half was in full swing while the beer continued to flow for the young rugby fans. They were delighted to share this moment with friends and couldn't count the pints. The Englishman then came back and insisted on Michael. This time, his answer was less categorical. He seemed to hesitate. The Brit sensed this and put £10 on the line. The argument finally convinced the Australian. "Well, it's going to happen," he said mockingly.

The first half came to an end. The challenge had to be met during the break. Hiding behind a human fence formed by his cronies, O'Brien undressed utterly. Socks included, that was part of the challenge! He then entrusted his belongings to two of his friends, who would wait for him on the other side of the pitch. To collect his £10, Michael had to cross the width of the pitch to collect his clothes from the other side or, at the very least, touch the grandstand.

While waiting for half-time, the Australian, bare as a bird's arse and fairly tipsy, waited for the opportune moment, lurking at the bottom of the stand near the halfway line. Then, the referee put his whistle to his mouth and finally blew the whistle for the break. Michael held his position for a brief moment, and as soon as the last players left the pitch, he took off.

What was he thinking at that moment? He would answer it himself, years later, in an interview: "I was blank to it, to be honest. From the minute I sent my clothes to the other side of the ground, and I was sitting there stark naked on the opposite side of the ground, everything just went blank. All I was waiting for was the half-time whistle for the players to leave the pitch."

No sooner had he stepped onto the pitch than a horde of stadium attendants set off in pursuit. But the young man was nimble and managed to keep them at bay.

The spectators who stayed in the stands during half-time would not regret having kept their seats. They were amused to witness an incongruity never seen before. Enjoying the distraction, they all began to raise their voices. Some cheered, others scorned the unexpected scene of nudity.

Surprised to hear this clamour from the crowd, Ian Bradshaw took a few seconds to realise what was going on. In front of him, just a few dozen metres away, a slim-looking young man with a full beard and half-length hair flowing in the wind crossed the pitch in its width. But it didn't stop there: this man was naked as the day he was born, his privates swaying with his strides.

The stadium attendants and the police joined forces in pursuit. The former steered him towards a human net set up by the latter, and Michael slipped into it without realising it.

The police were the first to grab O'Brien. Three officers overpowered him. One of them was Bruce Perry. The Bobbies vigorously, but non-violently, led the troublemaker off the field. It was then that O'Brien, firmly restrained, addressed the policeman Perry. He explained in a few words why he was on the pitch in Adam's uniform. He didn't forget to mention that he had to touch the fence to win his bet. And, as incredible and incongruous as it may seem, Bruce Perry let him hit his goal.

At the same time, Ian Bradshaw felt that he was potentially onto something big. He needed to capture the scene with his lens. He moved a few metres away and tried to catch the right moment to release the shutter.

It was a tricky assignment because the subject was naked. He had to manage to seize his best expressions and attitudes while not exposing his private parts.

Decency also drove Bruce Perry to search desperately around him for something to mask the young Australian's pride. Finding nothing in his immediate vicinity, he decided to take off his policeman's hat and held it in front of the young man's private parts.

Bradshaw didn't miss a beat. Without realising it, Bruce Perry was doing him a huge favour. "The thought going through my head was, "I wish that policeman would hold the bloody helmet steady because it bobbed up and down every time I pressed the button. All I was concerned with was, have I got the damn thing sharp and was the helmet in the right place?" recalled the photographer.

With O'Brien out of the sports field Ian didn't waste a second. He headed for his studio. And he never minded the end of the match! Right up until the final processing of the shots, he remained extremely anxious. Would he come out with a "decent" photo?

After drying, one shot stood out. This was the one that Bradshaw would submit to the Sunday Mirror. And it was this photo that would make him known in the four corners of the globe.

Michael O'Brien was shown almost full-frontal. Two policemen were escorting him along the touchline with a firm grip on his left arm. Despite this, the young accountant allowed himself to be led off the pitch without putting up any resistance. There was no hint of violence or animosity in the depiction.

The photo was published on the front page of the Sunday Mirror the following day, with the headline: "Well, it was a royal occasion". It would be picked up by a host of newspapers around the world. Since its publication, it has been used regularly in advertising campaigns. Ian Bradshaw made the first naked man to walk through a stadium at an official sporting event. The first "official" streaker in history.

Bradshaw received a £100 bonus for his excellent shot. The photo, which travelled around the world, would go on to win numerous awards, including *World Press Photo of the Year* and *Life Magazine Picture of the Year*.

But while the photographer was making the most of his sudden international fame, the model could have done without the spotlight...

After being escorted off the pitch and re-dressed, Michael was immediately taken to the local magistrate. He is fined £10 for "insulting behaviour". He, therefore, made no profit from his bet. However, the judge was kind enough to allow him to watch the end of the match. The procedure was straightforward, and the young Australian managed to get back to his seat to watch the second half.

Apart from a good laugh with his friends, a few hugs from amused onlookers and a fine, that was the end of the matter. Until the next day, when the photo was released...

In 2006, in one of the only interviews he gave, he said of his sudden celebrity: "If Ian Bradshaw hadn't got that photograph, it probably would never have happened. There were no TV cameras at the games in those days, so I would have had a clear run; nobody but the 48,000 people in the park would have ever known about it..."

With several decades of hindsight, Michael very much regrets this gesture. On other occasions, he would talk half-heartedly about the difficulties it may have caused when he set up his own business. But above all, he regrets having been at the origin of a wave of streaking, people with or without claims, who imitated him, interrupting hundreds of sporting events around the world."I do feel very, very guilty about that. The stupidity that went on for years and years later – and you just showed some of it – going onto live games, running onto racing tracks, it's just sheer stupidity."

Indeed, streaking will become commonplace. The phenomenon would only die out a few decades later. These demonstrations would cease when the television channels decided to stop broadcasting images of this kind in order to stop promoting and encouraging such acts.

During this famous interview in 2006, the journalist asked O'Brien if he had any advice for those who would like to emulate him. To which he replied: "Absolutely. Don't!"

21

1991: When the French national team almost went on strike!

France's run to the second World Cup ended in the quarter-final. The French left the competition on 19th October 1991 after a stormy match against eternal rivals England (England won 19-10). The match, described by some as an English trap, was marred by foul plays and dirty tricks on both sides, all with the blessing of the referees, who had clearly lost their visual acuity.

The last appearance of the legend Serge Blanco in the blue jersey left him with an immense sense of frustration and injustice. However, this missed quarter-final was only the pinnacle of an execrable situation within the French tribe. Behind the scenes, players, coaches and federation officials were at loggerheads for months.

It all began a few months earlier when Alain Ferrasse announced that he would not be standing for re-election as President of the French Rugby Federation. The battle to succeed him became so intense that the sporting side of things took a back seat. Expected in the United States for a preparatory tour, the French team found itself on the brink of standing up to its American hosts. With just a few weeks to go before the start of the tour, no one had bothered to organise anything or even to raise the necessary funds. In the end, Serge Kampf, one of the great patrons of French rugby, agreed at the last minute to sponsor the tour.

Once on American shores, the atmosphere within the group deteriorated fast. Performances that fell short of expectations and a generational conflict undermined Les Bleus' cohesion. The animosity even materialised physically when the *old* front-row - Ondarts, Marocco and Lascubé - came to blows with the young guard, Gimbert, Simon and Moscato, the flashy Bègles players who had just been crowned French champions.

On the return to France, the sporting results were respectable. A win against Romania, then two tests against the United States that the team won, and finally a victory in Cardiff against Wales on the way home. However, contrary to what the final results reflected, Les Bleus could not implement their system of play. The coaches - Jean Trillo and Daniel Dubroca - could not come to an understanding; the squad was constantly being reshuffled. For Pascal Ondarts, these reorganisations were the cause of France's failure at the World Cup: "How can you win games when, two months beforehand, you don't even know who's going to play?".

Dubroca finally took the initiative and published the list of players selected for the World Cup without informing Trillo. The former Agen's hooker made a clear-cut decision to resolve the generational conflict. He decided to put his trust in the old guard and to leave out the younger players, including the Bègles' players. Jean Trillo felt deeply betrayed: "I was disowned in the choice of certain players, and that created a climate of mistrust."

The World Cup was being played in Europe. The French national team enjoyed the advantage of playing all its group matches at home. Thanks to this major strength, the team won all its matches in the qualifying phase despite being on the back foot. The outcome was a ticket to the quarter-finals against England. Just as the group seemed to be on the right track, a new upheaval would rock it.

On the eve of the match against the Red Roses, the bonus promised by the Federation had still not been paid to the players. While the players had requested the tidy sum of 150,000 Francs per person (around €23,000), their supreme governing body only awarded them 7,000 Francs, or around €1,000.

The players then appointed their captain, Serge Blanco, to go and plead their case with rugby's big boss. "I would have played for zero cents, but I was the captain. The players wanted something in return for the time they spent on the French team. It seemed logical to me. Promises were made. They weren't kept. Money wasn't an end in itself. It was more a question of asserting a principle," said the Biarritz's player a few years later.

After being passed around between several executives, the French fullback, who was trying to raise the stakes, received a curt reply from Alain Ferrasse: "There won't be anything at all! If you don't want it, you can leave. We'll take another fifteen men, and that's that."

According to those close to Les Bleus, the squad simply threatened to go on strike and not play in the quarter-final against England. Eric Champ later denied this claim: "We would even have paid to play in this World Cup!" Once again, it was Serge Kampf who broke the deadlock at the last minute, signing 32 cheques for 200,000 Francs each (around 30,000 Euros), one for each player and member of the coaching staff.

Kampf would later say that "all the cheques were cashed. All except one, the one signed to Serge Blanco".

What followed was the same as rugby's great history: a 19-10 defeat. This was definitely not Les Bleus' World Cup. Even so, the great Serge Blanco would still have deserved a happier farewell...

22

Lawrence Dallaglio: The weaknesses of a champion

There is a category of champions among top-level players who are not content with merely reaching for the stars but conquering them all. Lawrence Dallaglio, former number 8 for London Wasps and the Rose XV is one of them. This breed of Lords is characterised by unwavering commitment, as well as an extraordinary passion, both on and off the pitch. It's an extreme character that, if left unchecked, can lead to certain excesses.

Lorenzo Bruno Nero *Lawrence* Dallaglio was born in London in 1972 to Vicenzo, an Italian immigrant, and Eileen, an Englishwoman of Irish descent. The hard-working Dallaglio parents instilled in Lawrence and his sister Francesca the values of hard work.

Educated at a Catholic primary school in Richmond (where he was also a member of the choir), Lawrence was introduced to rugby at the age of 8 during a mini-tournament organised by the school.

He then continued his education at Ampleforth, in North Yorkshire, also a Catholic school. Dallaglio still enjoyed playing rugby there, but on a dilettante basis, contenting himself with a place in the reserve team.

His life took a turn in 1989, with a slap in the face as a welcome gift to adulthood. His sister, for whom he was very fond, died in the tragic sinking of the Marchioness (51 people were killed when two ships collided on the Thames).

Traumatised, the Dallaglio clan pulled together to face this terrible ordeal. It was for this reason that Lawrence decided to return to London to live with his parents.

After successfully completing his secondary education, Lawrence enrolled at Kingston University in 1990. This choice was by no means random. The Kingston campus is located not far from the headquarters of Wasps RFC, the club with which the young man had decided to sign up. He would never leave the club and would experience most of the major events of his career with the London Wasps.

Three seasons after making his debut in the Wasps junior team, Dallaglio was called up to a senior team for the first time. This came in April 1993, at the first Rugby 7s World Cup. Although he was already a massive back row forward, his speed and agility were undeniable. These qualities enabled him to hold his own brilliantly in 7-a-side rugby, which is resolutely geared towards speed and elude. England, which played close to home (the competition was in Scotland), won the tournament by beating Australia in the final. The young Londoner contributed to the 21-17 victory by scoring a try.

In September of the same year, Lawrence first appeared on his club's first team. He played 12 games, including 10 as a regular, during the 1993/94 season. He quickly established himself and became an automatic selection the following season.

The end of 1995 marked a new turning point for the dashing young Dallaglio. Following the departure of a number of key players, he emerged as a leader, both on the pitch and in the changing room. At just 23, he took command of a squad that he led to 4th place in the Championship that season.

It was also in 1995, on 18th November to be exact, that he made his first England cap, coming on as a substitute against World Champions South Africa. A few months later, he won his first 5 Nations Championship for England.

The 1996/97 season saw Dallaglio crowned champion of England after a season dominated by Wasps, who showed a daring and dynamic running game. On the European stage, Wasps did not make it out of the group stages. They could, however, take pride in having inflicted one of their heaviest humiliations on Stade Toulousain: 77-17!

Everything seems to be going well for the Italian-born Englishman. The crowning glory for a British player came in June 1997 when he was invited to join the prestigious Lions on a tour of South Africa. And the honours continued to pour in. The following November, he was appointed by the staff of the Red and Whites to succeed Phil de Glanville as captain of the national squad.

In 1999, the Wasps captain collected a trophy that he did not yet possess: the RFU Knockout Cup. He also took part in his first XV World Cup.

The English team's elimination in the quarter-final disappointed him, but only a minor one in consideration for the rest of his career.

In fact, fate stepped up a gear in 2000. Another Tetley's Bitter Cup, then a (now) 6 Nations Championship, then a new 6 Nations Championship in 2001. No title in 2002. But Dallaglio and his national teammates sent out a strong signal by successively beating the All Blacks, the Wallabies and the Springboks during the November tour. They were a force to be reckoned with at the next World Cup.

Lawrence Dallaglio was also a force to be reckoned with in 2003: he pocketed a Grand Slam, which had eluded him for so many years, a European Shield and another English Championship. Finally, a few months later, the England back row forward was honoured with the Webb Ellis Cup, the crowning glory of a career and a year that had seen him win 4 titles!

His winning streak did not end with this major title. Wasps, led by a captain on the verge of becoming a legend, hit even harder. They completed the double Championship and European Cup in 2004, another Championship in 2005, an RFU Knockout Cup in 2006 and a second Heineken Cup in 2007.

In January 2008, Dallaglio announced publicly that he would end his career at the end of the season. Although Wasps suffered a poor start to their domestic league campaign, they gradually turned things around and qualified for the playoffs at the last minute. As a farewell gift, Wasps treated their legendary captain to a finish worthy of his career, an ending that every player would dream of. In the final, they overcame Leicester 26-

16, allowing the English back row forward to win his 10th and final title in the yellow and black jersey.

Unfortunately, his international career did not have such a happy ending. In 2004, after a half-hearted 6 Nations Championship, followed by a disappointing tour of the southern hemisphere (3 defeats), he decided to retire from international rugby. Asked to play for the Lions for the last time in 2005, Lawrence injured his ankle in the first match of the tour and was unable to finish it.

However, England coach Andy Robinson urged Dallaglio to return to action in the rose-embroidered jersey for the 2006 edition of the 6 Nations Championship. Dallaglio rose to the challenge, but England achieved their worst result in the competition since 1987, finishing 4th.

Lawrence was then no longer lining up for his national team. At least temporarily. After being sidelined for around a year, and with no one expecting to see him back at an international level, Brian Ashton surprised everyone by announcing that he had retained Dallaglio for the 2007 World Cup. "The commitment he demands makes the other players raise their game". This was how the coach justified the presence of the Wasps number 8 in the England squad.

At 36 years of age, Dallaglio's physical qualities had waned somewhat. As England progressed at the World Cup, Dallaglio gradually relinquished his regular place to the young guard, content to be a luxury substitute. However, his exceptional charisma had not changed in the slightest. His aura had remained intact and weighed heavily on the English team. It was undoubtedly one of the factors that helped the Rose Team reach the final of the competition. On 20th October 2007, Lawrence had the chance to win a 2nd world title against South Africa. He took to the field in the 65th minute for the last time in a white shirt but, unfortunately, could not turn the game around. This time, he had to be content with the second position.

Which trophy has Lawrence Dallaglio never won? None that he hasn't fought for. As well as being one of the few players on the planet to have won the 7-a-side and 15-a-side World Championship, he can also boast of having won every competition he has played in at least once. And, as an ode to loyalty, all of these honours (apart from the international titles) were won with London Wasps, the only team he played for at professional level for 15 years.

You don't build such a track record by chance. Not without a mentality of steel, a character that is hardened, fiery and committed. These attributes, which are qualities on the rugby pitch, can also prove to be weaknesses in everyday life. And who better than the British tabloids to exploit the slightest flaw in a high-profile personality?

Flashback. Dallaglio was appointed captain of the England XV in November 1997, at just 25 years of age, beating out Martin Johnson, then captain of the British Lions. But he was forced to relinquish the honour in 1999. This was due to the personal details he confided to Louise Oswald, a journalist with the *News of the World*.

The public quickly becomes convinced that the high-profile Londoner had been caught in what the English call a *honey trap*. A trap in which the sweet smell of sugar lures you but in which you end up getting stuck... However, the revelations made are no less resounding.

The News of the World had devised an obviously well-oiled and terribly effective ploy to extract some juicy anecdotes from the England captain. Louise Oswald had apparently begun to gravitate towards Dallaglio's inner circle, posing as one of his fans.

Having gradually gained the trust of her prey, she pretended to work for a cosmetics brand (using business cards and a fake email address), which was interested in using the rugby player's image. A lucrative advertising contract, with no less than £1 million up for grabs.

The sequel took place on 21st May 1999, in a room rented as a photo studio at the Conrad Hotel in Chelsea. A photoshoot featuring him with various bottles of shaving lotion was orchestrated by fake photographers. In reality, they were journalists from the *News of the World*. The atmosphere was intimate and hushed. Dallaglio would understand the reasons for this too late: the room was equipped with discreet microphones, and the journalists were trying to avoid interfering noises as much as possible. Complimentary glasses of champagne were served. Uninhibited by the alcohol, the Wasps back row forward let himself be talked out in the middle of a raucous conversation.

According to the British tabloid, he said: "I used to be a drug dealer. I made a lot of money selling drugs. How do you think I know so much about it? I was surrounded by dope. I used to drive from one end of London to the other with five or six ounces of cocaine. That's how I made money before rugby."

He then went on to confide in others: "I started using drugs again, cocaine and ecstasy, two years ago. After winning the Test series with the Lions (in 1997), we went on one hell of a binge. It happened in a presidential suite at the Intercontinental in Johannesburg. I was with two other players. It ended in the early hours of the morning."

Finally, Dallaglio confided about his strong attraction to the ladies. On this subject, he mentioned that he really enjoyed Amsterdam, which he discovered during a tournament he took part in. "There's forbidden fruit there," he said. He added: "Women are my Achilles heel."

The trap had worked perfectly. Certainly driven by the desire to impress Oswald and helped by alcohol, the English captain did not realise that he had literally thrown himself into the lion's den.

The revelations were made public in a first article on 23rd May by the *News of the World*, followed by a second on 30th May. The audio recording, however, was not released to the public but simply transcribed in writing. *The Mail on Sunday* also published an article accusing Dallaglio of being a cocaine addict, with witnesses to testify.

Unfazed by adversity, Lawrence Dallaglio decided to hold a press conference to justify himself in a transparency operation.

"I took drugs when I was younger, and I'm not proud of it," he said at the start of the interview. Then, on the subject of his misdemeanours during the 1997 Lions tour: "No drugs were taken on that trip. There are no drugs among the Lions. Regardless of the names thrown around by the media, I don't know any teammates who take drugs. I can't deny that certain reported words were said during that interview, but I categorically refute certain false allegations."

The Englishman regrets having been tricked like that by journalists and admitted that he went a little overboard: "I lied during the discussion with the journalists. I feel so humiliated admitting this today. I made up stories to impress them while following a line of questioning orchestrated by them. I never dealt drugs."

Then, on the road to redemption: "All I can do now is behave honourably, for the good of the England team and for my family. Rugby has given me everything in life. If I can get my career back on track, I will devote all my efforts to proving that I am a good player and, more importantly, a good person."

Dallaglio officially received the support of his club Wasps, as well as his peers, led by coach Clive Woodward: "I'm proud of the way Dallaglio has dealt with these allegations. The matter could have been settled by lawyers, but he prefers to be able to walk down the street with his head held high. He was simply stupid to have fallen into this trap."

Nigel Melville, Wasps manager and former England captain commented shortly afterwards that he 'understands, but does not condone' his player's drug use. But he added that it came 'at a difficult time in his life when he was destabilised by the sudden death of his sister'.

After the shock of the revelations, public opinion in England also turned in Lawrence's favour. While people do not condone the fact that the captain had taken illegal substances, they found the way in which the confession was extracted from him repugnant.

Final absolution was given the following August. The RFU report concluded that the party organised in the presidential suite of the Intercontinental was a pure fabrication. The Lions were staying at the Crowne Plaza on those days. The player's description of the premises to the News of the World seemed to be accurate, as he had previously stayed in several of the chain's establishments. All the presidential suites were laid out in the same way.

Accusations of drug use were also dismissed. No one other than Dallaglio had ever claimed or witnessed any such behaviour. In addition, all the Lions underwent anti-doping tests during the tour and, to this day, regularly undergo anti-doping tests.

Without exception and without the slightest doubt, they all tested negative.

In short, the only thing the England captain was found guilty of was lying, tarnishing the reputation of his federation, in order to secure additional personal income. As a result, the fine stood, but the player would be allowed to return to the national team.

The verdict was contested. The International Rugby Board considered that certain elements were overlooked by the RFU's disciplinary committee. The IRB pointed to the fact that, according to the investigation carried out by the English body, Dallaglio was indeed seen at the Intercontinental on the evening of the alleged offences. He was accompanied by two Virgin Atlantic flight attendants. They were, in fact, occupying a presidential suite. In addition, one of them knew some of the Lions players and had already attended Wasps matches. According to her statements, which she did not wish to repeat, a party did indeed take place in the suite she occupied. The festivities were very drunk, but no drugs of any kind were involved. The English criminal justice system was approached for a time but rightly replied that it had no power whatsoever over the adjudication of the facts.

Was the RFU trying to cover up for its now ex-captain in the run-up to the 1999 World Cup? Despite the doubts expressed by some, the story was dying down on its own, and Dallaglio was continuing his career, which would be the one we know.

As he had promised, he set out to prove that he was a good player, as well as a good person. Towards the end of his career, he began to get involved in events organised by various charities, such as Help for Heroes and Sport Relief. He also agreed to become honorary chairman of the Wooden Spoon Society, a rugby-related charity that helps underprivileged children. Also in 2008, following the death of his mother, Dallaglio set up the eponymous foundation to raise funds for the fight against cancer.

The name of the former captain of the England XV, the man with 85 caps, seemed to have been definitively rehabilitated and was now firmly anchored in the legend of rugby across the Channel.

However, in March 2020, his Achilles heel once again played a nasty trick on him. The London police raided a "brothel" in the Holborn district. The brothel was professionally organised and equipped with a credit card terminal. Thanks to the receipts issued by the machine, the investigators managed to determine that a card in the name of Lawrence Dallaglio was used to make payments of around £10,000.

The judge in charge of the investigation summoned the former rugby player for questioning. Naturally, the case once again made the headlines in the UK. It was being taken particularly seriously because, as well as offering the services of luxury prostitutes, the brothel was also known to sell various narcotics, including cocaine.

Transactions made from Dallaglio's credit card showed that some payments landed directly in the bank account of a prostitute; others were sent to the bank account of one of the organisers of the trafficking.

Those in charge of the investigations cautiously stated, at first, that there was no evidence to suggest that the payments were made by Dallaglio himself. Then, after interviewing him, they reported that he did not wish to comment on the nature of the transactions. There were no legal consequences because, in England, prostitution is not an offence, unlike procuring.

The Dallaglio case, or rather the cases, presented the British public with a dilemma that could be described as one of morality. While it may not be moral to use the services of prostitutes, and even less so to use drugs, should it be publicised in the newspapers and turned into a scandal? And, beyond that, is it a journalist's job to extract confessions through stratagems as elaborate as the one used against Lawrence Dallaglio in 1999? The debate remains open to this day.

23

1986: The battle of Nantes

In days gone by, the Battle of Nantes could have been the name of a decisive confrontation in the history of France. While the French city has indeed been the site of terrible battles in the past, the fight with which we are concerned is, in human terms, a very recent one. It took place in 1986.

15 warriors from a local horde, dressed in royal blue tunics and short white trousers, needed to clean their honour. Their collective honour. Facing them were 15 other sturdy men, all dressed in black. Their complexion was not indigenous; they came from the antipodes, and they were frightening. On 15th November 1986, the French national team and the All Blacks met for the second time in eight days.

The final score remains engraved on the official record. As for the match itself, it lives on in French memories as a reference point and an example of commitment. Because yes, the terrible All Blacks did fold. At the time, it was almost a feat. On the New Zealand side, some of the players were severely marked by the confrontation. Although usually fearsome, this team found itself cornered by a pack of 15 supercharged Bleus. Unstoppable. As if possessed.

For a match to become part of rugby mythology, it has to be held in Dantean circumstances. Different times, different customs, a hostile environment, men who stopped at nothing and no one. Fighting. A lot of fighting. Violence. And controversy has been constantly fuelled since then by additional 'stories', analyses, and complementary or... contradictory histories. Legends are always polished and magnified over time. Nantes 1986 is a perfect example.

Arriving on French soil in mid-October, the All Blacks are led by their most charismatic figures: Kirwan, Fox, Kirk, Fitzpatrick, Shelford, Brewer, Whetton... not a single one was missing.

They won the first 5 matches of their tour of France against various selections. On 8th November, they faced the French national team in the first of two tests. The teams knew each other well. During their last summer tour, France, winner of the 5 Nations Championship, had made a stopover in New Zealand. The Kiwis were uncompromising at home, winning 18-9.

The New Zealanders are hard to handle at home... and they export just as well! In Toulouse, they won the first test against France, 19-7. Each side scored a try. The French were well prepared and did not take this match as a joke. They battled valiantly but lacked assertiveness. Their visitors showed much more drive.

After the game, Alain Lorieux, France's lock, commented that 'we were chewed up'. Although this defeat was not a catastrophe, it did cause some nervousness in Les Bleus's squad. The first World Cup was fast approaching, and the group, held together by an iron hand by coach Jacques Fouroux, needed to reassure itself before the event.

Fouroux was much maligned by some in the world of Rugger. In a rugby culture still strongly influenced by the parochial spirit and clannishness, many reproached him for his choices. Nicknamed Napoleon, he perfectly reflected the image of his glorious ancestor. He brought a highly innovative vision to the coaching position, and with his stubborn, volcanic and even angry nature, he imposed his decisions against all odds. Suffice it to say he was not universally appreciated, particularly in the Toulouse region.

As a result, the Toulousan public completely turned a deaf ear to the match against New Zealand. Not much of a crowd, not much encouragement. In their own way, the locals made Fouroux pay for some of his selections. After this defeat, it felt like a debacle; the group was weakened. If it was not to explode, Fouroux had to find and bring in the binding force that the French team lacked. And just as well because Napoleon's imagination knew no bounds!

From Toulouse, each player returned to his home base. The following Wednesday, they were due in Nantes to prepare for the second test match.

The selected arrived at the Domaine d'Orvault in Nantes in dribs and drabs. They were greeted by Jacques Fouroux, who was in a bad mood, with a terrifying pout and a dark look in his eyes. In the days to come, he would only loosen his teeth to drown his team in more scathing admonishments.

Everyone briefly settled into their rooms and found that there was no electricity. No, because Fouroux had it cut off. He then switched on the main instrument of this preparation: a video recorder! The French didn't fail physically against the All Blacks; it was their minds that failed them. Napoleon, therefore, only had a few days to turn good players into bloodthirsty beasts. As usual, he was not going to pull any punches.

During endless video sessions, a highly unusual exercise at the time, Fouroux, who was as obnoxious and acidic as possible, put each of his players under the ground. 'We watched the match again, and every action, he stopped the video,' recalled Lorieux. Napoleon would lash out at everyone, whether for a tackle that wasn't hard enough, a scrum engagement that was too soft, or even for shaking hands with an opponent. With their minds compliticly messed up by their mentor's relentlessness; even the less fragile players ended up on the verge of tears.

Piquant as ever, Jacques Fouroux seized every opportunity to belittle his boys. He confronted each of them with their own personal demons, latching on to every psychological flaw he could spot. He knew their private lives and habits inside out and raked over the coals, their most sensitive points, without remorse.

Therefore, he reproached Jean-Pierre Garuet, the prop from the FC Lourdes, for eating too much cheese. He would simply have the cheese removed from the players' buffet. He also took the liberty of removing the wine. 'Which was really unusual at the time,' Serge Blanco later explained.

Meals were taken in dead silence. Everyone ate their meal in a hurry and disappeared from the dining hall. No one wants to cross paths with Fouroux. The simple fact of entering his line of vision meant exposing oneself to a salvo of scoldings. Jacques barked at anything that moves. The atmosphere he 'managed' to create was simply deleterious. 'If we came across him, we knew we were going to get the shit kicked out of us,' recalled Ondarts.

The technician, who was also a skilled psychologist, knew what he was doing. He used his method, which he followed to the letter. He wanted to make individualities disappear so that everyone had no hesitation in sacrificing themselves for the whole group. But he also knew how to slow down the build-up of pressure when the breaking point was near. He was also able to turn into a paternalistic guru who was close to his lads. He often slipped discreetly into the bedrooms of some of them, explaining, almost apologising, the reasons for his harsh decisions. He often justified it by saying, 'I had to do it'.

When the players of the French national team were asked about this preparatory period, the word that came up most often was "execrable". Denis Charvet: 'We had some great Jacques. He was terrible, indeed. He got us to a level of detestation we'd never seen before, so we had to be ready. Personally, I didn't hate him; I hated the situation.'

Indeed, he hit everyone's heads and imposed bullying and reprimands; the wizard succeeded in achieving his objective: his group was fired up, fuller up to the brim with hatred and resentment. Tension was at its highest. Everyone humiliated and wounded inside was emotionally (or even "mentally") groggy.

Late morning on Saturday 15th, the group set off for the Beaujoire stadium in Nantes. An electric silence, charged with tension, pervaded the bus. Not a word was uttered. After catalysing hatred and detestation, Jacques Fouroux had to urge his braves to release all this resentment on the pitch. The Little Corporal had his methods for that, too.

When the French entered the changing room, they didn't yet know that the devil was waiting for them there. The door shut to let the collective madness take hold of them. What they had experienced so far was nothing.

Jacques Fouroux handed out the jerseys to each person individually. He continued his work of dehumanisation. Always the same eagle-eyed gaze on them, one by one. What was he looking for in his players? Hadn't he already laid bare their every character trait, right down to the most profound?

He continued, ever more aggressive, with ever more hurtful words. Then, when the spirits were ready, and the hatred had reached its peak, he began the physical preparation.

Les Bleus would not see the grass until kick-off. The warm-up took place behind closed doors in the dressing room. Jacques even sent off the attendant, informing him that his team was due to be photographed. 'They don't deserve it!' he shouted.

He gathered his forwards. The eight lads formed a circle. Frail but proud, Fouroux slipped into the middle. They all looked dazed. All humanity seemed to have gone out of them. After another round of verbal abuse, Jacques suddenly, like a ram in a rut, headbutted his forwards in all directions.

If the first blow took them by surprise, no one was slow to throw the second. Like during a volcanic eruption, the guys unleashed a fiery cloud of blows on themselves. With their foreheads hot, they no longer had any limits. They slammed into each other hard and violently. 'Boom! Boom! Boom!' the headbutts were raining down. Fouroux remained in the middle and continued to transcend his troop with great slaps. He found himself caught in the midst of a herd of animals: animals that had gone mad, that didn't recognise themselves, that didn't even recognise their shepherd, who had become enraged himself.

The forwards, almost all bled, huddle together with their teammates from the back lines. In the confined space created, the smell of warming ointments saturated the atmosphere. Napoleon chose this moment to attack Philippe Sella. He pumped him up. He stretched him like a spring until the player could not stand anymore and, in a rage, threw him a masterly headbutt that left him half-stunned.

The craziness was contagious. They hit each other; they insulted each other; they didn't invoke the jersey and the country but the ties that bound these men together. Lobotomised by four days of mental destruction, they now formed a single body. A single entity inhabited by a devastating and destructive rage.

Denis Charvet, who made his first appearance at the centre of the French three-quarters line, recalled the almost unreal moment: 'It hit me! It hit me! I've been through a lot of preparations, but that was the most terrible.' For Frank Mesnel, 'That pre-match was a bit like taking on our opponents' trench'. There gave no quarters.

That day, FC Nantes footballer José Touré was invited by Serge Blanco to attend the pre-match warm-up. He had a front-row seat to watch this very special warming-up. He was a totally hallucinated witness to these scenes of preparation for battle. He would discreetly whisper into Charvet's ear: 'You're crazy, I didn't believe that could happen'.

After a preparation of unprecedented intensity and brutality, Jacques Fouroux opened the dressing room door, his face swollen, almost knocked out, completely dishevelled. Like a Roman animal master, he unleashed his furious animals into the arena. 'Bayonet to the canon', to quote prop Jean-Pierre Garuet, they headed for the field.

The starting XV has retained a specific backbone despite a few changes made by France's coach-guru. Toulouse's Erik Bonneval left his place at centre to Charvet and took his place on the wing. Franck Mesnel, who was naturally keen to play and open the game, was the orchestra conductor at fly-half. However, Fouroux had instructed him to use as many up and under kicks as possible. Lastly, Pascal Ondarts, after an interminable wait for the position, celebrated his first cap at the age of 30.

Everyone, beginners and experts alike, was over-motivated. They seemed to be in another dimension, their gazes electrified, their eyes exorbitant. When Wayne 'Buck' Shelford, the New Zealand number 8, met Les Bleus in the corridor, he was taken aback. These 15 Frenchmen didn't seem to be the same guys as the week before.

The same Shelford led the Haka a few moments later. His 14 teammates were forming an arc behind him, facing a French team that was united and resolutely ready for action.

Serge Blanco kicked off the game. The ball rose high into the Nantes sky. On the catch, the unfortunate Murray Pierce tumbled over and then trampled underfoot by the entire French train. The tone was set. The French, as if freed from the yoke of Fouroux, could finally let themselves go.

The strategy was simple: a physical tight play. Laurent Rodriguez: 'If we had the chance to make a pass... we wouldn't do it!'

Following this kick-off, France obtained two scrums, which led to a first penalty. Unfortunately for them, Bérot was not in the best of moods and missed the target. In general, the French scorers (Mesnel, Blanco and Bérot) would suffer the same poor performance, missing no less than ten attempts at points, penalties, drops, and conversions kicks together.

A few minutes later, the visitors decided to show that they were the best team in the world. The All Blacks set up a running attack, followed by a series of lateral passes, and reached the home team's in-goal... but failed to flatten.

This move was followed by a few temper tantrums, such as Brewer punching Condom in front of the referee or Champ overreacting to Fitzgerald. Then, on 19 minutes, Philippe Bérot opened the score with a penalty kick.

In the minutes that ensued, Kirwan made a delayed charge on Bonneval, who was catching an up and under. Champ and Shelford then sparked a brawl, which was immediately contained. The All Blacks finally broke the deadlock in the 27th minute with a penalty from Crowley. The New Zealand fullback would not be spared by the irregular tackles, particularly by centres Sella and Charvet.

Both sides exchanged ruckings and punches in the rucks like in kickboxing, which were punished... or not. Try this '18 stud! - Thanks, but you're not leaving France without eating leather from my shoe'.

A few minutes before half-time, on an eight-man push, the French scrum managed to carry the ball into the in-goal, but the try was not granted. In the action, Erik Bonneval wiped his studs on Wayne Shelford, but the gesture appeared to have been entirely unintentional. The New Zealanders then came under heavy defensive pressure and were forced to play in their own in-goal. They got out of this jam without any damage, and then each team went off to eat their lemons and orange quarters.

The first half turned in France's favour. The blue forwards did more than simply resist their All Black counterparts. They were the ones who imposed and won the physical challenge. The French were mastering the game thanks to a conquering pack like never before, administering wild rucks clean-ups.

About three-quarters, apart from the opening minutes, the New Zealanders struggled to make an impact. As for the French, they showed some fine intentions, but their clumsiness was to prove fruitless.

After the break, the away team began their assault on the French camp. Kirwan, who seemed to be back in business, made the difference, but the action did not go the distance. Then, because it had been a long time since there had been a foul play, Philippe Sella delivered a magnificent slapshot to Green. It wasn't for free, and it has to be said that it was the Canterbury winger who made the first move and elbowed Sella in the face.

The play resumed, and in the 50th minute, overlapped by Berbizier, Bonneval broke free down the wing. With 3 opponents just waiting to take a bite out of him, the Toulouse man improvised a football performance. He almost pulled off the perfect trick but pushed the ball a little too hard, and it went out as a dead ball…

It was now 57 minutes when New Zealand, with their backs to the wall, played a scrum 5 metres from their try line. Kirk put in the ball, but his forward bit the dust. Fitzgerald was unable to heel, and the leather ball was ejected from the scrum corridor. The ball was mishandled and fumbled... before being grabbed by Charvet, who sprang like the devil from his box and flattened the ball at the foot of the posts. The converted try was not the most spectacular ever scored, but it rewarded the French XV, who continued to dominate the game, particularly the powerhouse.

Wayne Shelford left the field just before the hour mark. He joined Whetton on the bench, who came off ten minutes earlier. Both would watch from out of the touchline, Philippe Bérot scoring another penalty, bringing the score to 12-3. Even though the All Blacks could have got away with a few of their trademark dazzling moves, the match did not look good for them.

The prospect of defeat loomed... and was confirmed. Erik Bonneval, who was definitely in form, was sent into touch just two metres from the in-goal. Hot scared in New Zealand's promised land...

Regular time was drawing to a close, but the French remained hungry for dessert. From a tap penalty, the forwards executed a set play well. They deceived their opponents and opened up a gap for Dubroca. The hooker broke through the defence and went to ground less than a metre from the goal line. In one move, Alain Lorieux lifted the ball and made the last effort to score the final points of the game.

16-3, the die was cast. Five more minutes to play, and then the three final whistles. And that was all. That was how this legendary match went and how it ended. There was no brawling, no general fight, no pitch invaded, and no players out of control. For the French, the match may be a milestone, but the legend was not yet in the making. It would only be afterwards, and only after analysis, that this match would finally be described as 'sulphurous', 'stormy' and even 'ambush' by the rugby community.

This is how this test match in Nantes, or friendly game, became known as the 'Battle of Nantes'. And as if to back up this judgement, the fate of Wayne Shelford on 15th November is always mentioned.

***

Born in Rotorua, in the northern part of the 'Land of the Long White Cloud', Wayne discovered rugby at an early age. He was then selected for the Bay of Plenty and Auckland secondary school teams. In the antechamber of the highest national level, 'Buck' demonstrated exceptional rugby skills. Tall (1.89m - 6.2 feet), athletic and tough, he was the very embodiment of the All Blacks' spirit. Resilient and determined, he never gave up. He never admitted defeat and refused to be tamed.

He pursued his rugby journey with the North Shore team from 1982. Shelford quickly attracted the spotlight and the attention of New Zealand coaches.

They offered him a chance on 12th October 1985. During a tour of Argentina, Buck achieved the ultimate honour for a Kiwi player. He wore the jersey emblazoned with the fern for the first time in a match against Club Atletico San Isidro.

Taking part in the controversial New Zealand Cavaliers tour in April and May 1986, Shelford was excluded from the All Blacks, like many of his teammates. The situation did not last, as the federation quickly absolved them. As a result, New Zealand could count on a fully revitalised team, ready for battle on their tour of France in 1986.

In the win at Toulouse on 8th November, the solid Aucklander celebrated his first selection in an official test by scoring a try following a big push from his pack.

Buck became a key figure in the number 8 position, and, obviously, he was selected to play in the 1987 World Cup. With a perfect balance between power and mobility, agility and solidity, he knew how to take part in the right movement. He showed himself to be decisive in the semi-final against Wales, scoring two tries, including one in the second minute of play. The following week, Shelford would lift the Webb Ellis Cup.

In the aftermath, he also picked up the Bledisloe Cup with a hard-fought victory over Australia in Sydney. Highly committed to his team, Shelford took over the captaincy from David Kirk. Under Shelford, the All Blacks would remain unbeatable.

After taking another Bledisloe Cup in 1988, the Blacks hosted - and dominated - the French on their 1989 summer tour. They then crushed the Pumas in two more tests and retained the Bledisloe Cup. Even away from home, New Zealand remained untouchable.

On a tour of Canada and the British Isles, nothing and no one was able to challenge the Blacks' dominance. The British Columbia selection, the Welsh clubs, the Irish provinces, the British Barbarians, the Irish and Welsh National XVs... Everyone bit the dust, and the Kiwis came out on top: 14 wins from as many matches played.

Although unanimously acclaimed as captain, Shelford suddenly found himself disowned by his coach, Alex Wyllie, who had confidence in him since the start of his tenure. Buck would be blamed, not for any defeats, but for two victories over Scotland that were deemed to have been too sluggish. Not wanting to acknowledge that the Scots had fielded a generation of talented players who had won the Grand Slam, Wyllie deposed Wayne from captaincy as well as the selection.

The public got terrible upset and angry. Everyone remained convinced that Shelford was the captain by excellence because of his dedication, human values, and skills as a player. New Zealand's opinion was all the more heated because no clear explanation had been given by the management of the All Blacks. It was rumoured that the manipulation behind the scenes was orchestrated by the Auckland contingent of players, who wanted to establish their province's dominance within the national team.

The affair gradually spread beyond the universe of rugby. At public events of all kinds, placards demanding the skipper's return sprang up, all bearing the famous slogan: 'Bring Back Buck'. The resentment was further exacerbated when the Wallabies won in New Zealand in August 1990, ending a run of 23 Tests without defeat.

Popular pressure did nothing. Wyllie would not reverse his decision, making Buck captain of the All Blacks unbeaten in official matches. In his 25 months as captain, and with 14 official Tests played, the Kiwis had never lost. On a personal note, Shelford only lost once in 22 Tests: on 15th November 1986.

After a consolation prize of a return to the national side and the captaincy for hosting Romania and the USSR in 1991, Wayne bowed from international duty. In 48 matches, including 31 as captain, he scored a total of 22 tries.

Shelford then decided to change the scenery and moved to Europe. He breathed new life into the Northampton Saints squad, which needed a leader, and ended his career in Italy with Rugby Rome at the age of 38.

In addition to his rich sporting career, Wayne is also renowned for his involvement in promoting the Haka. With his deep respect for this ritual he had helped to give it the status it occupies today.

Wayne developed a keen interest in the Haka very early on, during the first tour he took part in. The topic is close to his heart, unlike some of his teammates. The ritual dance was even so anecdotal for some of the team that the idea of no longer performing it before matches was mooted.

Shelford refused to accept this. So he got together with hooker 'Hika' Reid and organised a vote. Their teammates had to answer the following question: Does the Haka still have a rightful place before matches?

The vote was in favour. A "yes" that simply meant that everyone agreed to get more involved in understanding and performing this Maori (war) dance.

Indeed, until then, it was clearly visible that a majority of 'Pakeha', non-Maori players, were executing approximate gestures. What's more, some players were only superficially aware of the spirituality surrounding this practice. For Reid and Shelford, if the Haka was to be performed, it must be done perfectly, and its meaning must be clear.

Grabbing hold of the subject, Shelford made approaches to the Maori leaders. He got them to allow the All Blacks to come and immerse themselves in the indigenous culture of New Zealand. These interactions strengthened their understanding of the Haka and, above all, taught them how to perform it without error. And to put this teaching into practice, the team would even have special training sessions dedicated to this signalled code.

Wishing to perform the ritual on New Zealand soil (until then, it had only been performed at away matches), Buck was one of the first to raise the subject with Maori elders and opened the door for discussions. As a result of these rapid negotiations, the ritual has been allowed to be practised on New Zealand land since 1986.

As Buck's influence grew in the late 1980s, the controversy around 15th November 1986 swelled. Theories and uchronies are all based on the sad fate that befell him. Freshly buried bodies were dug up and autopsied in public.

The extreme engagement of the French, with a great deal of supposition and extrapolation, was portrayed as pure brutality, as gratuitous violence. For Berbizier: 'It was portrayed as a sulphurous match. When you watch the match again, yes, it was a hard-fought match, but it was oversold afterwards. Shelford overdid it.'

Indeed, Wayne would become the main character in the post-match drama that is still being played out regularly over the decades. Partly canonised by his people on the altar of the suffering he endured on 15th November 1986, Wayne regularly and publicly revisits that day. Each time, his words are repeated and often distorted before being broadcast.

More and more evocative and extreme words are used. However, the excessive use of the lexical field of violence, even war, is abused.

As Berbizier said, it was a hard-fought and committed match. Yes, the French cleared the way in all directions, arriving with 10 metres of momentum, cab forward, looking to dismantle the New Zealanders. Admittedly, there were some bad acts. But it has to be said that both sides administered rucking, trampling and other underhand strokes. By Serge Blanco's own admission, 'Yes, we did throw a few dogpiles'. There was no doubt that the French, in the promiscuity of the clusters, settled a few accounts. However, the images show that the All Blacks were undoubtedly the quickest to draw their weapons. Let's not forget that Shelford himself was known for his willingness to take the law into his own hands. And it showed in this match.

As the 4 days of French preparation in Orvault gradually unfolded in bits and pieces, there were rumours of a 'contract' for the heads of Whetton and Shelford. This claim was always denied outright by the French. Perhaps they simply rammed and trampled indiscriminately, injuring Whetton and ripping the unfortunate Buck to shreds. While the former escaped with a lesser injury, the latter paid for his presence at La Beaujoire with his own blood. And almost lost some of his manhood in the struggle.

During this match 'which he remembers but doesn't want to watch again', before the 20th minute, Wayne found himself in an unfortunate position in a pile-up of players. Chastised by the blue forwards, he lost a couple of molars. But that was not the worst of it. Indeed, Buck felt a flow, which turned out to be particularly badly localised.

The All Blacks' medic couldn't believe his eyes. On removing Shelford's shorts, he notices a gaping hole in his scrotum. Worse than that, a testicle was exposed to the air, held together by just a few fleshy strands. Wayne claimed that Dubroca 'raked his privates'. The French hooker had always said he 'doesn't remember'.

This was the point at which Shelford became a legend. He asked the doctor to suture his scrotum... and returned to the field after pouring a little water on his shorts. At that moment, no one had any idea what had just happened.

Without giving anything away, the back row forward held his ground and seemed set to play this match to its conclusion, despite his condition. But it was without counting on the blows of the French helmets which got the better of him. He was sent off in the 58th minute. It would be discovered later that he was a victim of concussion. Rainy weather for Buck. However, his courage and resistance to pain earned him boundless admiration from the public.

In the press, from one article to the next, between omissions and inaccuracies, the episode of the martyrdom of the hero Shelford was gradually becoming blurred. With this disjointed tale still with us, supported by period videos, all of them truncated, some journalists have come to dispute Shelford's version.

First of all, they make a point that is not insignificant: while Wayne describes having lost his molars (3 or 4, depending on the source), we never see him bleeding from the mouth. Did he not bleed? Did he rinse his mouth out off-camera? Did he really lose 3 or 4 molars?

Secondly, and again, based on the videos available today, there is no image of Shelford being trampled. Wayne says he was injured around the 20th minute, while journalists focus on Bonneval stepping on the All Blacks in the 38th minute. However, on some of the tapes, Dubroca can be seen 'slapping the arse' of Shelford as he sits on the ground. This effectively happened around the 20th minute. And when you consider that this grandfatherly method is intended to put the testicles 'back in place' after a shock, Shelford doesn't appear to have been lying. What's more, a key witness in the person of Brian Lochore, attested to the injury: 'I nearly threw up. It was the most horrible thing I've ever seen on a rugby pitch.'

Another element that contributed to the legend and to the doubts of some concerns was the treatment of this delicate injury. Some articles detail that the unfortunate Wayne was quickly stitched up on the touchline; other accounts mention that the stitches were applied in the changing room. Still others tell of a brave Shelford, who waited until half-time to get stitches and played injured for the rest of the match. Nothing is more uncertain than where the operation took place. As for the fact, reported by many newspapers, that Shelford had finished the match, nothing could be further from the truth! As we know, Buck came off in the 58th minute. But this assertion so magnifies the story that it is often adopted.

About his final knockout on the grass at La Beaujoire, Wayne himself is muddying the waters. He asserts and maintains that it was Garuet who knocked him out. He insists on one important detail: the man who beat him up was wearing a blindfold. But Garuet didn't wear any scrum cap. Lorieux was wearing one. And it was indeed Lorieux who had a field day with Buck.

Wayne's words, though staggering and with a few exceptions, appear to be true. As for this outburst of violence, so often portrayed, it's just an imaginary generalisation of the Shelford case, which, it's true, had a hell of a time that day.

In another dimension altogether, one that many are reluctant to mention, the match has remained in people's minds because it is regularly cited when the scourge of doping in rugby is mentioned. For Wayne Shelford, the French were doped. When he came across them in that famous corridor at La Beaujoire, he was almost frightened: 'Their eyes said they had taken something, and I couldn't prove it'.

In the 2000s, with only his conviction to support his arguments, Buck spoke out on several occasions in the media. He hammered home the point that his opponents were 'under-substances', but always with his own feelings as the only evidence. Given the halo surrounding the former Blacks skipper, his words are like gospel. The fact that the French XV were doped was, therefore, a proven fact for some.

However, as Wayne points out, no proof was ever provided. At the time, just after the Nantes crushing, the New Zealand coaching staff lodged a complaint with the IRB. The Kiwi staff also requested that the investigations be carried out discreetly, as the use of doping products is a highly sensitive subject to handle.

The investigation provided no answers to the accusations. Speculation will remain at this stage, probably forever. Despite the context and the questions that remain unanswered, one can only conclude that Shelford's reputation as a gentleman has not been usurped. In spite of all this, he nonetheless declared: 'We mustn't take anything away from the French, who completely dominated us that day'.

The Battle of Nantes was once again brought to light in 2015. French journalist Pierre Ballester, who specialises in the study of doping in sport, published a bombshell of a book: *Rugby à Charges*. The publication literally divided rugby's French world and generated violent reactions. With good reason, Ballester reports on institutionalised doping in the French team at certain times. To back up his investigation, he relied on information provided by Jacques Mombet, the official French national team medic between 1975 and 1995. And according to the doctor, the match in which 'it' was most obvious was... the 1986 Beaujoire match!

In *Rugby à Charges*, the doctor revealed an explosive piece of information: 'At mealtimes, each player had his (amphetamine) pill next to his plate'. A number of prominent figures came out of the woodwork, taking up the cause in favour of the book. For example, former prop Laurent Benezech, who had already been denouncing these practices for some time: 'Taking drugs in rugby was comparable to the doping practices in cycling'.

The clan of the French national team at the time, including the coaching staff, denied the whole allegation. Some felt hurt by such suspicions, as it was related to one of their fondest memories as a player. Others came to the defence. The FFR retorted that anti-doping tests had been carried out since 1982, and not a single player had tested positive, 'or even suspected'. The federation also asserted that, at the time of the alleged events, Dr Mombet was never in contact with the team. What's more, he was not present at the Domaine d'Orvault during the preparations. For Ondarts: 'When you spend a week locked up with Jacques Fouroux, you don't need to be doped up to go into battle! I wouldn't wish it on my worst enemy...'.

Others, notably Philippe Sella, were taking legal action. The former Agen centre received a letter of apology from Doctor Mombet. In this letter, Dr

Mombet stated that the information had been taken from him rather than given willingly. Were his words distorted after they had been taken? Jacques Mombet is no longer here, but the book of the Battle of France remains open so that the legend can continue to be written.

For France, this victory, this reference match in terms of commitment, is without doubt the consecration of the Jacques Fouroux method. Unfortunately, this game became the catalyst for his defeat in the World Cup final the following year.

Frightened that their dominant position could falter against a resolute team, the All Blacks had just enough time to restructure before the first world tournament kicked off.

In December 1986, John Hart and Alex Wyllie succeeded Tiny Hill and Collin Meads at the helm of the Kiwi national team. They brought with them Jim Blair, a physical trainer whose methods were futuristic but highly effective.

When the New Zealand squad watched the France-Australia semi-final, everyone was rooting for the French. They were still offended by that defeat at La Beaujoire. They all wanted to play Les Bleus in the final to make amends. On the day of the final, manager Brian Lochore, who had been there on 15th November, put up a sign in the dressing room at Eden Park with just two words: 'Remember Nantes'.

'We wanted revenge and to prove that we were better,' said Shelford. Their revenge is called the Webb Ellis Cup.

24

1973: A 5 Nations Championship with no losers... and no winners

In 2017, the way in which points were counted for teams taking part in the 6 Nations Championship was changed. Since then, a win is worth 4 points, and a draw 2 points. Offensive and defensive bonus points were also introduced. These were added to an existing system to count the difference between points scored and conceded in matches (the goal average). With the arrival of this new mechanism, it is now virtually impossible to have a perfect tie between two teams. But this has not always been the case.

On 13th January 1973, on a grey and cold day, Walter Spanghero's French team hosted their Scottish counterparts at the Parc des Princes. It was the kick-off to the most intriguing 5 Nations Championship in history.

France beat Scotland that day 16-13.

Unlike today, the days of the Tournament are not all held over the same weekend. They were spread out irregularly between mid-January and mid-April. So it was not until the following week that Wales beat England 25-9 in Cardiff.

On 3rd February, Scotland and Wales played their second match at Murrayfield. The Scots won 10-9, thanks to two tries from Steele and Telfer. Ireland, who had not yet played, began the competition on 10th February, defeating England at home.

24th February was the only day on which all the teams played a match. The French lost in England, while the Scots triumphed once again at home against the Irish, 19-14.

At the tournament's halfway stage, Scotland was top of the 5 Nations Championship with 4 points, including 2 wins, all at home. The other four teams sat in second position, with 2 points each.

After a two-week break, the competition resumed on 10th March at Cardiff's Arms Park between Wales and Ireland. AJ Lewis' team-mates won 16-12 at their home ground.

Scotland and England played their final match on 17th March at Twickenham. The Thistle boys could not seize the opportunity to secure a final victory. The English, in great shape, scored 4 tries, giving them a 20-13 victory. After the match, the day's two opponents both found themselves in first place in the competition, level with Wales. But unlike Wales, England and Scotland were no longer in control of their own destinies.

The Dragons, for their part, could still claim to be in the hunt for overall victory if they travelled well to France the following week. Unfortunately for the Welshs, the hero of the day was Jean-Pierre Romeu, wearing the blue jersey. By scoring all 12 of his team's points, he kept his rivals in first place, albeit on a par with England, Scotland and France.

The "final" of the 1973 5 Nations took place on 14th April between Ireland and France. Both teams had a lot at stake. An away win for the French would see them crowned champions, with 3 wins in their pocket. As for an Irish victory, it would lead to an unprecedented situation: a perfect tie between the 5 nations of the tournament.

The green full-back Tony Ensor opened the scoring in the first half with a penalty kick. It was not until the 48th minute that centre Mike Gibson doubled the score. But just as it looked like the home side would win, winger Jean-François Phliponeau stepped up to the mark, scoring a try in the 78th minute. Unfortunately for Les Bleus, the conversion failed to go over the posts, confirming Ireland's victory.

With this latest victory, the most improbable scenario was validated. With each team having won its two home games and lost its two away matches, the 5 nations were perfectly even on points. Based on the goal average, Wales was in first place (+10), followed by Ireland and France (tied at +2), then Scotland (-4) and finally England (-10).

However, the rules at the time did not allow the rankings to be based on anything other than the number of points won (victories or draws). As a result, there was no designated winner, and all the teams were crowned victorious!

At present, with the introduction of bonus points, such a tie would be hard to envisage. And even if it does, the new rules would allow the total goal average to be examined, followed by the number of tries scored and conceded, and then the number of cards. It is, therefore, certain that the outcome of the 1973 5 Nations Championship will forever remain unique.

25

Record in the land of the rising sun

When you think of the most prolific try scorers for the national team, the first names that spring to mind are the *aliens* of planet rugby, such as Bryan Habana, David Campese and Doug Howlett. However surprising as it may seem, the record for tries scored for the national team is held by a Japanese, Daisuke Ohata.

The Japanese player, an unrecognised record holder, was born on 11th November 1975 in Osaka. At the age of 9, he chose to play rugby rather than baseball, one of Japan's national sports. Uncomfortable interacting with those around him, he found in this sport, as he puts it, "a way to express himself".

From an early age, he stood out for his impressive speed. This asset, which he cultivated and improved throughout his career, enabled him to excel in the art of evading defences and outrunning his opponents.

In 1991, he joined his high school (Tokai High School) team before moving on to Kyoto Sangyo University in 1994. Positioned on the wing and occasionally in the centre, Ohata always shone with his rapidity, complemented by an acute understanding of the game.

The supersonic winger was quickly spotted and appeared in the Japanese squad for the 15th Asian Rugby Championship in 1996. He came on as a substitute in the tournament's final, which he won against South Korea, winning his first international award in the process.

Promoted to captain of his Kyoto Sangyo team, he led his teammates to the Kansai championship title in 1997. In the process, they knocked out the formidable Waseda University 69-18. After qualifying for the National University Championship, the Kyoto team lost in the semi-final to Kanto Gakuin University of Yokohama.

In 1998, Daisuke Ohata then signed for the Kobelco Steelers, part of the Kobe Steel company, based in the city of the same name. Then, in October, he competed in and won another Asian Nations Championship.

Already a 15-a-side international, the Japanese winger was also included in his country's 7-a-side squad for the famous Hong Kong tournament in 1999. There, he gained his credentials in the sport, notably by outrunning the entire Scottish defence to score a try from 100 metres. Although the Japanese team was competing for the *Plate* (a trophy at a less prestigious level), Ohata was crowned best player of the tournament. This had never happened before for a player competing in the *Plate*.

Back at 15, wearing the colours of the Cherry Blossoms, Daisuke Ohata scored one of Japan's only two tries of the 1999 World Cup against Wales. Unfortunately, although the Japanese battled hard, they could not win any of the matches.

Despite struggling to triumph against major nations in the years 2000-2010, the Japanese national team dominated Asian rugby across the board without exemption. And it goes without saying that Ohata, spearheading the team, gave many opponents a run for their money. During qualification for the 2003 World Cup, for example, he scored a whopping 8 tries against Taiwan, setting a new record!

Although he came from a championship and a national team that were not very visible, the winger from Kobe was nevertheless spotted by a French club, AS Montferrand, in 2002. But the experience was not a happy one and turned out to be short-lived. After playing just 2 French Cup challenge matches in early 2003 (but scoring 4 tries in the process), Ohata rejoined his club Kobelco Steelers. Officially, he could not get his licence validated, as the quota of two non-European players had already been reached by the Auvergne-based club. But there were persistent rumours that the Japanese player was suffering from terrible homesickness.

Disappointed at not having been able to make his mark in France, the Nippon wing three-quarter would be determined to give his very best to take his team to the top at the 2003 World Cup. The Braves Blossoms' results were encouraging. Although they again failed to pick up a single match, they confirmed their progress, as well as the growing strength of their team. Daisuke Ohata added 2 tries to his tally.

The winger, still on an upward trajectory, had the privilege of winning the first edition of the Top League, Japan's elite championship, with his club Kobe in 2004.

Then came his finest hour, the pinnacle of his career, on 14th May 2006, during a test match between Japan and Georgia. In the 36th, with his speed still as sharp as ever, he flattened the ball behind the line after following a kick ahead distilled by Yuta Imamura. Then, just before the hour mark, he rallied to join his forwards in a penetrating maul that propels him into the Georgian in-goal. Finally, in added extra time, following a touch inside the opposition's 22, the player scored his 3rd try of the game.

Scoring a hat trick against a strong Georgian team was an achievement in itself. But Daisuke Ohata had just smashed another, far more prestigious record. With 65 tries scored in 55 internationals, the Japanese player has simply beaten the world record for the number of tries scored in international matches by one. The previous record was 64, held by an Australian, a certain David Campese...

Smiling as he was leaving the dressing room, but nevertheless very humbled, Hoata told the press: "I doubt that David Campese ever thought that his record would be beaten by a Japanese. I felt a sort of pressure on my shoulders. I'm glad I did it". He concluded with a very Japanese formulation, very respectful: "In a way, I feel sorry for having beaten David Campese's record".

However, when you are in the spotlight, you can expect to see the other side of the coin. Some Western media, including the BBC, preferred to be detractors rather than given praise. Statistically, David Campese scored 64 tries in 101 caps, while Ohata scored 65 in just 55 appearances. Journalists sparked controversy by insinuating that only 25% of the tries scored by the Japanese had been against major nations. Some also revised the statistics, using complex calculations to decide whether a particular nation is a major rugby nation or not. Then, the controversy died down because the figures were there and cannot be denied.

Daisuke Ohata wasn't stopping there. He was only 30 years old, and his career was still going strong. However, although his points tally continued to climb, the rest of his career would be filled with major physical issues.

At the end of 2006, in the Top League, the newly-crowned record holder suffered a ruptured right Achilles tendon. He spent the first part of 2007 in rehabilitation. He made a sparkling comeback in August, scoring another try in a match between the Cherry Blossoms and an Asian team. But two weeks later, during a World Cup warm-up match against Portugal, his left Achilles tendon snapped.

It was a sad time for Ohata, who dreamed of leading his team to at least one World Cup victory. He had to watch the competition from the stands and would not be present for the draw with Canada.

More than ever, eager to extend his trophy cabinet, Daisuke enjoyed a fine 2008/09 season with Kobelco Steelers. But as fate would have it, he suffered a dislocated shoulder in the Top League semi-final and lost to Toshiba Brave Lupus.

The Japanese Shinkansen came to another halt, this time for good, on 9th January 2011. Just as his team narrowly missed out on qualification for the Top League play-offs, his right patellar tendon ruptured. Operated immediately, Ohata decided a few days later not to return to the pitch and retired for good.

With 69 tries in 58 caps (including 55 as a regular), the Japanese is still, at present and for a number of years to come, the reigning record holder for the number of tries scored in international matches. He is ahead of Bryan Habana, David Campese, Shane Williams and... one of his compatriots, Hirotoki Onozawa. In their respective countries' colours, they touched down 67, 64, 58 and 55 tries respectively.

Since then, Daisuke Ohata has made a few appearances on television shows. In 2016, he became the second Asian player to be inducted into the IRB *Hall of Fame*, joining another Japanese, Yoshihiro Sakata.

After being named ambassador for the 2019 World Cup, the record-breaker simply said that he wanted "the Japanese people to be able to explore the magnificent mindset that surrounds rugby, to immerse themselves in the sport and attend at least one match, whether they know the rules or not."

When asked to recall his most poignant sporting memory, he did not refer to his 69 tries: "At the 1999 World Cup, on the day of Wales-Japan. Although the match wouldn't kick off until the evening, I opened my bedroom curtains early and was impressed to see a veritable tide of people dressed in the red of Wales. I told myself that the World Cup really did have the power to move an entire country."

Humble to the end. The humility of great champions proves that despite his detractors, Daisuke Ohata is well and truly in his rightful place at the top of the try-scoring charts.

26

24 February 2007:
The English "back" at Croke Park

Following on from article 5 about the return of rugby to Croke Park, the build-up to the match between Ireland and England at the same stadium on 24th February 2007 took place in an emotionally charged context. The decision that the stadium would host a rugby match (a *British* sport) between the Shamrock XV and France's Les Bleus on 11th February 2007 was coldly received by the public. But the England match two weeks later opened some historical scars.

Since Bloody Sunday in 1920, the pitch at Croke Park has been banned from all *foreign* sports by the GAA. In January 2004, the project to modernise the Lansdowne Road stadium was finalised. It would prove to be a mammoth task, as the venerable Dublin sports stadium would have to be razed to the ground before being rebuilt. The Irish capital would thus be temporarily deprived of a venue for major sporting events.

The football and rugby federations then turned to the GAA, asking it to agree to make Croke Park available to them for certain matches. The request met with a favourable response from Sean Kelly, President of the

GAA. However, he was unable to give his immediate approval. The ban on non-Irish sports on the pitch was written in black and white in the association's rules. A paragraph, the 42nd, had to be voted on and added by the GAA's executive committee to revise the institution's operating rules.

Although Kelly wanted to be openly progressive, he came up against certain peers in the Gaelic organisation, who were conservative and fiercely opposed to a vote on the motion put forward. Supporters on both sides would campaign for several months, unleashing passions both inside and outside the GAA.

In April 2005, the Council of the Gaelic Athletic Association convened at Croke Park for a vote. Sean Kelly's initiative required more than two-thirds of the votes to be approved. Despite the doubts and uncertainty, the motion eventually passed by a wide margin. The President of the GAA could only savour his success.

However, some of his opponents would hold a bitter grudge. Kelly would deal with teething problems: "I'll never forget coming out of a shop and being greeted by a passer-by who said, 'You bastard! You're going to let the English into Croke Park!' There was another person who disappointed me enormously. He was a former leader of the GAA. A very respected person. One day, he refused to greet me, saying to my face that he wouldn't shake hands with anyone who brought the Anglo-Saxons into Croke Park. I also received many unpleasant letters and phone calls. Some weren't so brave that they preferred to share their views anonymously."

The opening of the Dublin stadium to foreign sports would bring in a tidy sum for the GAA, in the region of a million euros. It was interesting to note that none of the counties, even those most fiercely opposed to the YES vote, refused to take their share of the cake.

In 2007, a few weeks before the opening of the 6 Nations Championship, the controversy, largely fanned by the press, resurfaced in full force: "Is playing a rugby match in this stadium sacrilege? Or a step forward?" Once again, public opinion was unleashed and torn apart.

In a bid to calm the situation, Chris Ashton, the coach of the Red Roses, called a gathering of his players and their future opponents. Some Irish internationals, close descendants of former IRA fighters, took the floor to explain to everyone what that terrible day of 21st November 1920 was like.

Despite this, the media storm redoubled in intensity. Two days before the match, JJ Barrett, a great Gaelic football player of the 1960s and now an influential writer, demanded that the GAA return his father's medals. His father had also been a Gaelic footballer and had played an active part in the country's independence. He later donated some of his decorations to the Croke Park Museum. For Barrett Junior, it was simply inconceivable that *God Save the Queen* should be played in this stadium.

Finally, the day of the match arrived. The English fans were greeted by a few tags and vehement banners brandished by some of the Irish: "Don't say sorry, say goodbye" and "Brits out". Kelly once again took the blame. His name was associated with that of Judas on several placards waved by demonstrators.

The world of rugby also kept a close eye on the pre-match. Everyone was waiting for the national anthems. What would the public's reaction be when the English anthem was played? Would the crowd erupt in bitter booing? Or Would they respect the moment?

The two teams lined up, and then, in honour of the visitors, the orchestra into the first notes of *God Save The Queen* in a stunned silence that lasted until the end of the tune. No one in the audience showed any animosity. The Irish anthems followed, among the most poignant in the history of the Tournament, moved many spectators and players, such as hooker Jerry Flannery, to tears. Joël Jutge, the match referee, recalls that he himself was overcome by the emotion of the moment.

Ireland eventually won the match by a score of 43-13. On 24th February 2007, the two nations, once enemies, were certainly reconciled a little more. And it was rugby, above all, that won the day.

27

1990: The world's most beautiful anthem is born

All national teams and the people and supporters behind them are thrilled when the national anthems are played before the battle begins. Some of these even resonate with rugby enthusiasts across borders. Such is the case of the Scottish anthem, *Flower of Scotland*, which is considered by many to be the most beautiful anthem in the world. Even if you don't have a drop of Scottish blood in your veins, it sends shivers down your spine every time it's played.

The story of its birth, or rather of its official use, is closely linked to the Grand Slam won by the Thistle Boys in 1990. Behind that achievement were men with generous hearts who needed a strong symbol to topple a mountain and make their people proud.

In 1990, Scotland had 2 Grand Slams to its name, won in 1925 and 1984. And in Edinburgh, it seemed that the alignment of the planets was just right to win a third. With David Sole, Derek White, Craig Chalmers and the Hastings brothers, the Thistle XV had a solid and talented backbone.

The team, which would go on to play in a World Cup semi-final the following year, was probably one of the finest Scotland had ever fielded.

Expectations were confirmed when the Scots entered the competition. They bravely won in Ireland, 13-10. Two weeks later, Sole's team put in another strong performance, beating France 21-0 at home. Then, on 3 March, after another narrow 13-9 victory over Wales at the Millennium Stadium in Cardiff, the whole of Scotland found itself on cloud nine. All that remained was one more step towards the most prestigious, albeit unofficial, European title.

However, the final hurdle in the quest for the Holy Grail was England. And overcoming them would be no mean feat! The Red Roses, led by Will Carling, successively dominated Ireland at Twickenham 23-0, France 26-7 at the Parc des Princes, and Wales 34-6 at home.

The Thistle and the Rose would go head to head in what would be a real final. The stakes were high: the Triple Crown (awarded to the British team that manages to win all its matches against the other British nations), the Calcutta Cup (awarded to the winner of the England-Scotland clash) and the ultimate trophy, the Grand Slam of the 5 Nations Championship.

Before the match, the Highlanders were by no means favourites. Although the clash was scheduled to take place at Murrayfield, and the English were rested on Matchday 4 of the tournament (due to an odd number of participants), an analysis of the performances of the two teams favoured the Whites. The Scots would have to sublimate themselves and find that extra bit of spirit to beat their arch-rivals.

David Sole, a skilled prop as well as a charismatic captain, decided to take matters into his own hands. He began by imposing radio silence on the media in order to, as he put it, 'let the English get carried away themselves, or be carried away by the press'.

The group's silence was only the first step in an operation in which Sole had the trump card up his sleeve. To carry out the rest of his plan, he would have to use his powers of persuasion and activate every possible lever. And with good reason: the Scottish captain was planning, no less, to have the Scotland XV adopt a new national anthem! What better occasion than this match against the English? Especially as, until now, his team was represented by... *God Save the Queen*!

The track earmarked as a potential anthem for the Scottish national team, or even the Scottish national anthem, was already found. It is *Flower of Scotland*, a song composed by Roy Williamson, a member of the Corries, a traditional Scottish music group.

Written in the mid-1960s and popularised in 1967, the song is an ode to the Highland glens and the cream of the Scots warriors (the flower, or fine flower). They routed the invaders from perfidious Albion at the Battle of Bannockburn in 1314. Several centuries of independence for the Kingdom of Scotland followed.

At the end of the 1960s, Scottish populists tried to impose this tune as the official anthem - or at least unofficial - for Scotland's cultural exchanges and sporting events. The Queen of England, Elizabeth II, issued an outright veto. She judged that several lines in the first verse denigrating Edward II, her distant forebear ("Proud Edward's Army" – "And sent him homeward" – "Tae think again").

In 1974, during a tour of South Africa by the British and Irish Lions, *Flower of Scotland* was taken up by the Scottish fans who had travelled there. Over the years, the song became an ever more important part of Scottish sporting folklore, right up until the mid-1980s.

At this time, *God Save the Queen*, which was also supposed to represent the Scots, was increasingly derided by them. To prevent the situation from escalating, the Corries' song was finally authorised, at the request of the sports federations, to be played before unofficial matches.

Delving into the inner circle of the 1990 Thistle XV, we can discover the extent to which the Scottish history to which this song refers would be a catalyst in the conquest of the Grand Slam. Hooker John Allan recalled: 'We used to sing *Flower of Scotland* in the dressing room before matches. But we'd never been allowed to sing it on the pitch before. I knew it was important, but I didn't realise how important it was.'

Allan continued: 'On the Thursday before the game [against England], we all watched the Rob Roy film together. After the part of the film where the English soldiers massacre a clan made up entirely of women and children, our coach, Jim Telfer, jumped out of his seat and said to us: 'Look! If you don't kill those bastards, they'll kill your children and take your women'. I realised then that this would be much more than a rugby match.'

The following evening, the team attended a concert by Ronnie Browne, the original singer of what would soon become their anthem. That night, he sang the melody several times, dedicating it to them. Each time, the audience was thrilled and electrified, singing at the top of their lungs.

Finally, Saturday, the day of battle, arrived; a day of glory, it was hoped, in the clan of descendants of the brave Scots. At the end of the morning, Jim Telfer asked the forwards to join him in their training gear at a stadium not far from the hotel where they were staying. They complied and saw they were not alone when they entered the field. The forwards of the local club, Edinburgh Wanderers, were waiting for them, dressed in England jerseys. Telfer shouted: 'We'll only beat the English this afternoon if we can destroy those guys this morning!' Backrow forward John Jeffrey tried to argue against this, saying that these players were Scots, brothers, and they wouldn't be able to do that. One of the Wanderers coldly replied, in a strong local accent: 'We're English. Kill us!' The two packs would go at each other for a good half-hour, wrecking the stadium grass in the process!

In the afternoon, as the Scots arrived near Murrayfield, their bus faced a packed crowd. Thousands of supporters had come to cheer them on. Some were dressed in blue, others wore kilts, and still others were frantically waving flags. As the bus made its way through the mass of people, in slow motion, one of the players started humming *Flower of Scotland*. Everyone immediately imitated him. The moment, as only a pre-match can offer, was unbearably emotional. 'I looked around me and, at the back of the bus, I saw some of the toughest players with tears in their eyes and their heads down. I knew then that we had more than talent; we had a passion and a reason to win,' recalled Telfer, still overcome with emotion.

In the changing rooms, after the warm-up, bandages were adjusted and ointments applied. The bodies were ready for confrontation. All that remained was to prepare the spirits. Telfer enthused his troops, reminding them how important the match would be. For them, of course, but also for the whole nation that would be cheering with them that afternoon. Then David Sole asked everyone to sit down on the floor close together. He had already won a fight. Everyone would be able to sing their national anthem in the pre-match. He spoke calmly, like a reassuring skipper: 'Today, your body doesn't belong to you, it belongs to the nation. Our compatriots have been denied the right to officially sing their national anthem. Today, for the very first time, they are going to do it. And they are going to do it for you. All I want is for you to make them proud.'

The English took the field, confident and focused, but convinced that they would bring the Grand Slam back to London. *God Save The Queen* was played first, in honour of the visitors. Then, after a short silence, the first notes of snare drums and bagpipes echoed around Murrayfield. Would the public follow?

The audience responded enthusiastically, singing with ardour a song that would now become officially their own.

The outcome, a happy one for the brave Highlanders, is well-known to all. 13-7 to Scotland, who won their third Grand Slam and, as of now, are still waiting to win a fourth.

In 1993, the Scottish Rugby Union decided that *Flower of Scotland* would be played before every Scottish national team match. In 2003, a petition was initiated by the politician George Reid, demanding that the Scottish anthem, judged to be too vindictive towards the English neighbours, be replaced. The request, judged not to be a priority, was rejected. Then, in 2006, another petition was launched by Chris Cromar, calling for the song to be made the official anthem of the whole of Scotland. Parliament again rejected this request on the grounds that 'it is not for politicians to provide the country with a national anthem'.

In 2008, before the Scotland-France 6 Nations Championship match, the bagpipes suddenly fell silent before the second verse, leaving a huge choir of supporters to fill Murrayfield stadium with their fervour. After that, the initiative became a habit: every time the Thistle XV played at home, the second verse was systematically sung *a cappella*.

For the record, at the end of the 1990 match, the Scottish players kept the English and Scottish officials waiting for over an hour. They had all gone to a small pub on the stadium's outskirts to offer their supporters beers. Most of them were simple workers who could not afford tickets to attend the match. In the manner of their warrior ancestors who, a few centuries earlier, had made an entire country proud, they decided to commune with their people by repeatedly singing *Flower of Scotland*, a song inspired by a glorious past. A glorious past that resurfaced on this Saturday.

Printed in Great Britain
by Amazon